Whining & Dining

Emma Waverman
& Eshun Mott

Photography by Jenna Muirhead-Warren

Whining
& Dining

Mealtime Survival for
Picky Eaters and the
Families Who Love Them

Random House Canada

Library and Archives Canada Cataloguing in Publication

Waverman, Emma
        Whining & dining : mealtime survival for picky eaters and the families who love them / Emma Waverman & Eshun Mott ; photography by Jenna Muirhead-Warren.

ISBN 978-0-679-31454-7

        1. Cookery.   2. Food preferences in children.   3. Children—Nutrition. 4. Children—Nutrition—Psychological aspects.   I. Mott, Eshun   II. Muirhead-Warren, Jenna   III. Title.   IV. Title: Whining and dining.

HQ784.E3W39 2007   641.5'622   C2006-905695-1

Text design: CS Richardson
Typesetting: Andrew Roberts

Printed and bound in China

10 9 8 7 6 5 4 3 2 1

Contents

I like ketchup.

Tomatoes not so much.

Introduction
Perfection Is Not on the Table

Your kids are happily sitting at the table. As you set out tonight's meal, they all murmur their approval and dig right in. They reach eagerly for the vegetables and even agree to try your new, kid-friendly dish of chicken curry. They ask for seconds and don't even mention dessert until it arrives at the table. STOP THE MUSIC! If this is your house, then you don't need this book.

However, if your dinner table is full of chaos and whining, if you are worried that your children are not getting the basic nutritional building blocks for a healthy life, if the path between the table and the fridge is worn out because you've become a short-order cook, if the word "YUCK!" is being said too often, then keep reading. You are not alone.

Other Words for Picky

- challenging
- choosy
- discerning
- fussy
- *#@!!!

Ah, the irony. We—Emma Waverman and Eshun Mott—are both food professionals, making our living by cooking and writing about food, and, yes, we are the parents of picky eaters.

Like you (we assume, since you've cracked open this book), we have dumped plates of food into the garbage. We have lied and cajoled, and we have also capitulated and served our kids only the foods they like. When we've witnessed other people's children eating broccoli and tofu as snacks, we have silently cried in the corner. We each have awoken in the middle of the night in a cold sweat, worrying that our kids are going to grow up to be sickly, skinny nerds. We have called ice cream a meal and bacon a protein—more than once.

Our mothers watch with dismay as we cart boxed macaroni and cheese to family occasions. They remind us (subtly, they think) that *we* were never that picky and cluck disapprovingly about our kids' table manners. We like to remind them that life is different now—working parents and elaborate family dinners don't always mix. And we are quick to point out that, these days, parenting is a different business. We sanctimoniously throw around the term "child centered" and feel quite good about our parenting skills. And then we sit down to the table and become different beasts altogether.

If you are reading this and have a ten-month-old happily eating kale and lentils, don't be smug. Around their first birthday kids often start eating less, and around age three, they start using food (as well as everything else) as a control mechanism. Welcome to the world of picky eaters.

The Daily Grind

Feeding a family day after day can be exhausting and emotionally draining, especially if you find yourself facing a picky eater. Sometimes it seems as if no one else could possibly be dealing with the same insanity that you are encountering in your home. Well, craziness comes in many guises, and we have been there—we've heard the stories (and told quite a few too). After talking, whining and commiserating with other parents, we decided it was time to share our collection of ideas and tips for making mealtime an enjoyable experience. Some will work for you and some will not—it depends on the child. And because kids are unpredictable, some will work for a week and then never again. But we are confident we're offering an approach that will ease your mealtime stress, as well as some fantastic, simple yet flavourful recipes.

We are food lovers—and, yes, we are discriminating (but don't you dare call us the P-word). We want our kids to embrace the vast and delicious variety of foods out there. We want them to be able to find joy in eating, as we have, and to understand that food is one of life's simple and enduring pleasures. We also want to be able to enjoy all the other lifelong benefits that eating together as a family can provide.

Two busy parents, several kids, soccer games—it seems close to impossible to fit a family meal into our hectic timetable (and we can't begin to imagine how single parents tackle this task). But we are starting to believe that there *are* ways to adopt more food-friendly routines and that we *can* feed our kids healthy foods they will eat. With small but important changes to our daily routine, kids can begin to learn to trust their bodies and to choose food that is delicious *and* good for them.

In the end, despite the yelling, we cannot force our kids to eat the foods *we* want them to. The only thing we can control is the food that goes on the table. Then we have to let them have control over what goes in their bodies. The good news is that despite their diets and our worst fears, our kids still grow. They have lots of energy—sometimes too much—and are bright, engaging, inspiring little people.

This book is not for people who are aiming to be perfect parents. We understood a long time ago that perfection doesn't happen at the dinner table. And after all, there will be at least three more chances to do it right tomorrow.

Reasons to Appreciate Your Picky Kid

- You always know what's for breakfast, lunch and dinner.
- Shopping lists can be recycled week after week.
- You always have the perfect excuse to get out of unwelcome dinner invitations.
- You can escape to the kitchen during family occasions to prepare your child's "special meal."
- In a world where most people don't get enough to eat, a picky child is a reminder of the embarrassment of riches that surrounds us.

Broccoli, huh?

Chapter 1
How Did We Get Here?

So how did we get here? How did our tables turn into battlegrounds? We would like to blame the kids. How many times have you said, "They're just naturally picky"? And that's true, but we also know, and all the professionals tell us, that we played a role as well. Did we put too much emphasis on food? Yes. Did we give our kids too much control? Yes. Was it a mistake to throw a party because they ate green vegetables? Yes.

Picky eaters have an uncanny ability to make mealtime no less than a living hell, three times a day, seven days a week. You don't want to be there, and guess what? They don't either. Unfortunately, you are the adult, and it's your job to create an atmosphere that will encourage the consumption of some sort of food. The good news is that although most kids go through a picky eating phase, most of them also grow out of it.

In the meantime, how are you going to tame this mealtime madness? You won't want to hear this, but if meals are a nightmare and your kids are picky, it's your fault. Maybe not 100 percent your fault, but you played a big part. And the worst thing is that it's your fault because you *cared*. You probably made them "kid food" because you thought that's what they wanted. And now that's all they will eat. All that worrying and fretting about how to get your kids to eat taught them that they are in control. Or maybe you took all the control away from them and forced them to eat what you considered a healthy dinner.

In fact, most issues around the table have very little to do with food. It's all about power. Your kids are choosing not to eat that fabulous dinner you made for them because it gives them power over you and control over their own lives—something they so desperately want in this formative time in their development. So you have to take the power out of the equation. How do you do that? You have to give up some of your power. More on that later.

Why Are Kids Picky?

Let's be fair to kids. Every day they are bombarded with new experiences, new information and new expectations. They are foreigners in a land where everyone else knows what's going on. And to expect them to eat unrecognizable food every single day may be too much for them. It's like backpacking through an exotic country and having to trust the locals that you are eating chicken and not cobra heart. After a while, you too would cling to what you know.

Almost all children go through a picky stage. In fact, research shows that thirty-six months is the height of pickiness. It even has a scientific name: neophobia, the fear of new things. Scientists haven't figured out why kids go through this, but it may have been an anthropological means of protection during hunting-gathering days. Now, of course, the new scientific definition is "pain in the butt."

The good thing is that researchers have not found any connection between picky eating and adult diseases, or a lack of growth. However, eating habits that are taught in childhood—good ones or bad ones—can last a lifetime. If your picky eater is only picking junk food and sugar, you need to nip that habit in the bud. Obesity is a disease that has links to childhood. Studies show that in most cases you can limit and even prevent childhood obesity by providing healthy food choices, encouraging an active lifestyle, and teaching kids to know when they are hungry and when they are full.

A child's personality can also play a role. Kids who have trouble with transitions, who do not adjust well to new environments or people, are probably not going to be the kids who like to try new food. But if your little ones are always the first to run up to the crowded slide and make new friends, they may also be more adventurous at the table.

Eating is just part of your daily routine, and if you're dealing with a picky eater, you may want to look at mealtime behaviour within the context of what else is going on in your child's life. Is there a new baby on the scene? Has your child started at a new school or with a new

Books About Food for Picky Eaters

- *Green Eggs and Ham* by Dr. Seuss
- *Bread and Jam for Frances* by Russell and Lillian Hoban
- *Garbage Delight* and *Alligator Pie* by Dennis Lee
- *D.W. the Picky Eater* by Marc Brown
- *Voyage to the Bunny Planet* by Rosemary Wells
- *The Very Hungry Caterpillar* by Eric Carle
- *One Hungry Monster* by Susan Heyboer O'Keefe
- *Eating the Alphabet* by Lois Ehlert
- *The Seven Silly Eaters* by Mary Ann Hoberman

HOW DID WE GET HERE?

caregiver? Are there changes in the daily routine? Any change can affect how children behave, and in order to cope, they will aim squarely at an issue you find important (like their diet).

You may have one kid who eats everything and another who hates everything, just to be different. Siblings are forever defining themselves in opposition to each other, and food is just another realm in which to do that. Is chocolate one kid's favourite? Then the odds are on vanilla for child number two. Are you giving one kid lots of positive attention for eating and then giving lots of negative attention to the pickier child? This won't be easy, but as a parent you must resist comparing your kids and saying things like, "But look at Sammy eating his broccoli—what a good boy!" It's only going to make things worse. Really.

Kids have natural likes and dislikes, and we have to respect that. We allow that our partner may not like cauliflower, so why do we feel the need to force-feed it to our three-year-old? Some kids prefer salty, some sweet, and some kids will naturally avoid anything bitter. Sometimes kids will instinctively avoid foods that disagree with them without realizing why they're doing it. So keep your eye out for patterns that may be linked to intolerances.

Other than that, it comes down to you. Take a moment and reflect on your own attitudes. How do you feel about food? Do you use it as a system of control? Do you put too much emphasis on it? If your meal is rejected, do you take it personally? Do you nag your children and obsess about every morsel they eat? Do you obsess about every morsel you eat? Is your self-image as a parent partially riding on what they eat?

If you answered yes to any of these questions, go directly to a therapist . . . just kidding. Most of us have some emotions tied up with food, and we pass them on to our kids. Remember, kids will use anything they have to get attention, and most kids don't care if that attention is positive or negative. Being picky is a great way to get attention, often lots of it.

So here's the hard part: don't give it to them.

Bad Memories
"One of the worst conflicts I had with Zachary was when he was just over three. He wanted to be fed all the time. He would not lift a morsel to his own mouth. Eventually, I had a total breakdown, screaming and yelling. After I had calmed down, we worked out a deal: for one week, I would feed him breakfast and lunch but dinner was up to him. After that, the food would be put in front of him and he would have to feed himself. Then I said nothing else about it. In hindsight, I realize that the issue had more to do with the arrival of his baby brother than it did with food."
Emma

Just Throw It in the Fire

"My oldest son Max's standing breakfast request was 'a peanut butter English muffin sandwich, really crunchy and a little bit burnt.' And if the English muffin wasn't crunchy enough, Max would choose hunger over an imperfect breakfast. This seemed extreme until I realized that I prefer my toast on the crisp side and wouldn't want someone to get it wrong. And then I thought about how powerless Max was to get what he wanted to eat, and I decided the least I could do was make his toast the way he liked."

Eshun

The Long and the Short of It

You need to change your focus—think about your long-term goals for your kids, not the short. We're going to assume that one of your goals is for your kids to be able to make healthy choices for themselves. We want our kids to know when they are hungry and when they are full. We want them to understand that food nourishes the body and the soul, and that healthy food will make them feel good inside and out. And we would like to be able to sit at the dinner table with them and not want to pull our own hair out. And to do that, we may have to change how we approach mealtimes, and how we react when our kids don't eat. But don't worry, this should cut down on your workload, not add to it.

This is a process. And if you suddenly change the way you behave at the table, at first your family may look at you like you're crazy and react negatively. When they realize you are serious, they will come around. This may take weeks, or even months, but it will be worth it.

The most important thing to remember is that it's your responsibility to make good choices available—and then let your kids choose what they'll eat, and how much.

Starting right now, resolve to prepare ONE sit-down family meal every day.

Here is the rest of the plan to tame mealtime madness and get your picky eater eating a variety of foods.

- Arrange structured meals and snacks.
- Stop nudging, pressuring or commenting on what the kids are eating.
- Quit being a short-order cook.
- Stop bribing, yelling or punishing.
- Create a pleasant mealtime environment.
- Write up family rules that everyone can live with.

Whose Body Is It?

If you have a preschooler, you have probably heard the phrase, "You are *not* the boss of me." In a sense, your child is right. If we want our kids to grow up to make good choices for themselves, why would we force-feed them? They need to learn when they are hungry and when they are full. And they need lots of practice making choices before we send them out into the world of mass-marketed junk food.

We'll say it again: It is the kids' job to eat when they are hungry. It is your job to give them healthy choices. That's it. Close the book now.

Still here? Hooray! Then let's recap. As the parent, you are in charge of what is in the fridge and pantry and what goes on the table. The kids can decide for themselves what to eat from the healthy choices you give them. That means if they only want to eat mashed potatoes for dinner and ignore the roast chicken, they can. And if they want to pick the bacon bits out of their Caesar salad, ignoring the healthy lettuce part, they can. And if they want to ignore all the delicious choices that you have lovingly prepared for them, they can do that too. And you will say nothing and you will *not* take it personally.

You can show them what a healthy meal looks like by eating one yourself. You should trust them to make good choices for themselves, even if they are only two years old, even if they are so skinny you think the wind is going to blow them away. You have to trust your kids to make healthy choices for their own needs. And you *can* trust them, because you raised them. Does this strike fear in your heart? Of course it does. But there is actual science behind this theory. Studies have shown that over a one-week period, kids will eat everything they need for proper development, as long as they are given healthy choices.

Kids are like animals—they eat when they are hungry and have an innate sense of what their bodies need. We just need to have faith in our little wild beasts.

Hunger Is Punishment Enough

In talking with other moms and dads, we have heard about a few draconian measures some parents have undertaken to get their kids to eat. We do not think it is appropriate to force your kids to eat with an egg timer ticking by the plate, or send them to their rooms because they won't eat Mom's meat loaf, or feed them their uneaten dinner for breakfast. If your kids do not eat their meals, then isn't being hungry punishment enough? Take the challenge and tap into your creativity— you *can* feed your kids without humiliating yourself, or them.

The Family Meal

The one thing we kept coming across as we read and researched was the importance of the family meal. In the past, when our friends told us their kids weren't picky, we thought, wow, they are so lucky! Now we realize that it's more than luck. For the most part, they are the ones sitting down and eating together as a family on a regular basis. The children are never given control of their menu, and their parents do not make separate meals for each child. The result is that mealtime is not just about food; it's about being part of a family.

This does not mean the kids eat everything that is served to them. Most kids will pick and choose; they will whine and complain; they will only eat bread. The point is that the focus is not on what the kids eat. The parent removes the emotional issues around food; the food is served, and everyone digs in. Since mealtime is not a power struggle between the parents and kids, the kids don't choose the dinner table as an arena for fighting, and in that reverse-psychology kinda way, the kids are more likely to eat. Here is one of those parental truths: the more fighting there is at the table, the less your kids will eat.

So our very scientific study comes down to this: eat with your kids. This is not always going to be easy—we know life is not a Norman Rockwell painting. Life, work, commitments—they all get in the way of families sitting down together. So think outside the box: Does a family meal have to be dinner? Can it be breakfast? Emma's family makes a point of eating together on the weekends; Eshun does a family meal five or six nights a week. Of necessity, some families feed the kids early and then the kids join the parents later for a dessert or a snack while the parents eat their dinner. The message is the same: mealtime is family time, a satisfying experience that everyone looks forward to.

Sometimes it's only Mom or Dad who sits down with the kids; sometimes it's a caregiver or grandparent. But the meal is a social occasion. It's

Been There, Done That

Georgia, a preschool teacher, has been serving lunch every day for eight years and has noticed a few things.

- Kids will eat almost any vegetable raw, even ones they would never touch cooked.
- At the beginning of the school year about half of the students reject her hot lunches, but over time every kid will eventually sit down and eat the hot meal.
- In all the time she's been at the preschool, only a couple of kids have routinely rejected every meal. And even those kids have energy to spare.

a time to reconnect and talk about the current playground crisis; an opportunity to tell jokes and make silly noises; a place to learn some manners and feel like part of a family. Kids are keen social mimics, and the family meal not only teaches them about your attitude towards food but also about the world in general.

The benefits go far beyond getting your child to eat spinach. Studies have shown that teens who eat with their families on a regular basis are less likely to smoke, drink or use drugs, and are less susceptible to depression. And it has also been proven that adolescent girls are less likely to fall into that scary realm of eating disorders if they make an appearance at family meals. Eating together is a habit that is worth starting early.

Family-Style Eating

Whenever possible, try to serve one meal, and one meal only, and serve it family style. This is when all the dishes are put in the middle of the table, and family members serve themselves. The kids can take as much or as little as they want. Sometimes a gentle reminder that the green beans are hiding behind the dish of rice is acceptable. For younger kids, we may put a small portion of all the offerings on their plates and they can eat or reject what they want. They can always ask for more of any item.

The caveat here is that there is always something on the table every kid likes—even your most difficult eater. Often, that means some kind of plain starch such as rice, pasta or bread, and a fruit or vegetable (one deemed acceptable by your picky eater) or even yogurt. You can make "kid meals" occasionally too, as long as you don't label them as such. You may find that chicken fingers actually taste good when you are not eating them every day. Of course, there are days when you are too tired

Air Supply
"My kid is an airitarian. Good thing air is nutritious."
Leslie

Is It a Power Struggle?

Your internal temperature is reaching combustion levels, an earth-shattering yell is building and you have a compulsive feeling that you have to win. You are in a power struggle. Power struggles are more about winning and losing than about whether your kid is eating their dinner. Battles at the table will only make picky kids pickier because they don't want to lose either. You need to create a situation where everyone feels like their voice is heard and some of their needs (no matter how ridiculous) are met. Then and only then will peace reign at the table.

to cook, or you are craving something hot and spicy that the kids won't go near, and then it's time to pull out something fast and easy for them.

The table will not be such a threatening place if the kids know there will always be *something* they like. They may not be happy to have plain rice for the tenth time with no "kid food" in sight, but if they are hungry and/or bored enough, they just might try the main course. This is an exercise in trust—if they trust that you have thought about them and their preferences, they may in turn start to trust that the things you are eating are good too.

The Short-order Cook Is on Strike

This bears repeating: If your children are all over the age of one, then it is one meal for the whole family. No running to the fridge to make a quick sandwich, no caving in for mac and cheese. There is one meal on the table. There can be variations within that meal, of course. Maybe one kid will have plain pasta, one likes pasta with a little sauce and the third eats the whole dish of pasta with sauce and some salad on the side.

You will have to see what works best for you, but this is an important rule to follow in principle. Some parents allow the kids to have a yogurt or bread and cheese with the meal. Or after dinner the kids can make themselves something simple (emphasis on make *themselves* something) like a bowl of cereal. What you do not want is your kids thinking that they live in a restaurant where they can order up whatever they want, no matter what time of day it is.

Take a Break

If things get crazy at the table, you don't have to send the kids away. You can take *your* meal somewhere else. Bathrooms have locks for a reason. Don't think of it as a sacrifice; think of it as going to your happy place.

Structure Holds It Together

An important part of this approach is making meals and snack times predictable for the whole family. Meals and snacks should be approximately two to three hours apart and *never* withheld. Even if your kids do not eat the main meal, we think they should get a snack a couple of hours later. It's a safety net for them—they will learn that even if they don't like what is served for a meal, they will not starve. This takes the anxiety out of rejection and, surprisingly, may actually make them more open to trying new foods. And don't forget that snacks are an important part of kids' diets—their stomachs are just too small to eat enough at one sitting. What kids eat is a lot more important than when they eat it. Snack time is also a low-pressure time when children will often wolf down healthy foods without even thinking about it. (See Chapter 6 for yummy homemade snacks.)

Hungry children are not happy ones; you don't want them to come to the table, or go to bed for that matter, with a vendetta.

Say Goodbye to Bribery and Bargains

Your kids are not donkeys; holding a carrot (or a piece of chocolate) out in front of them will only work for so long. Stop making dessert the only reason to eat dinner—it puts too much emphasis on the sweets and makes the rest of the meal seem like drudgery. This may sound counterintuitive, but if you've planned a dessert as part of the meal, then you must offer it as an option for everyone at the table. It should not be used as a bargaining chip so that Junior will eat that bite of chicken. That said, if you only offer child-sized portions, Junior will soon learn that eating *only* dessert is not an option—because hunger will surely follow. (See Chapter 9 for more dessert tips and delicious recipes.)

Funny Things Kids Say
"If you don't give me something to eat for a long time, my tongue forgets what it's like."
Zachary, age 6

Define "Picky"

When asked if his five-year-old son, Jordan, was a picky eater, Richard replied, "Picky? Picky assumes that there is *choice*. That he will actually pick something!"

And please, no begging—it's embarrassing. If you manage to force them to eat that one bite of eggplant, they are not likely to choose to eat it tomorrow night. In fact, they may never choose to eat it again.

Rules of Engagement

Lest you think we are advocating a complete live-and-let-live attitude, we do have some rules that your children—and you—should follow at the table. These may differ from family to family, but here are some good ones to keep in mind.

She Knows What She Wants

Solaia, a notoriously picky eater, was eating lunch at a friend's house. When her friend's babysitter set down some berries in front of her, Solaia looked up ever so sweetly and said, "Didn't anyone tell you that I don't eat fruit?"

- No saying "yuck" or making other disparaging remarks about the food. If you don't like it, don't eat it.
- When you are done, you say excuse me and you can leave. (This is best for kids over three—younger than that and there is a bit of come and go.)
- You do not have to stay at the table waiting for everyone to finish. (This rule is actually a bonus for the parents—boredom leads to bad behaviour.)
- No toys at the table.
- No fighting.

And here are a few rules for the adults.

- No lectures or recriminations on any subject, including the kids' eating habits. The table is not the place for this.
- No discussing how hard you worked for the meal—although you can let the kids know that compliments on the meal will be gladly accepted.

- Keep it light, informative, maybe even fun. Make your kids want to be there because it's a relaxed way to connect, not because you've tied them to the chair and lectured them about antioxidants.

You have to be clear about the rules of the table, offering subtle reminders when necessary. Discuss the rules with your kids sometime when you're not at the table, post them and—this is the most important point—stick to them. Your kids can even offer some suggestions. Make them feel they're part of the process of making mealtimes enjoyable for everyone.

Getting Picky Eaters to Try New Things

Even though you are now suspending all negative behaviour at the table, your picky eater may still not be trying anything new. Have patience; it will come, eventually. Sometimes smelling is the first step, sometimes licking, and sometimes taking the teensiest bite imaginable. Even spitting something out is a good sign—at least there was tongue contact! Do not give up. Once the atmosphere around the table is one of acceptance and trust, your kids will gradually try new things without fear.

Be aware that while you may be making baby steps at home, you should not expect that your child will start eating more adventurously while in other environments, like family occasions. Grandma may have to wait a while before seeing Junior eating something she made for him. While you can't control the outside world, try to let family and friends, and anyone who may be looking after your child around mealtimes, know of your new approach in the hopes that they will back off on the begging and bribery too.

Research has shown (yes, someone is in a lab right now offering Brussels sprouts to three-year-olds) that a child may need between six and

It's perfectly normal if your child:

- cannot stand one drop of mess on the table, chair or shirt but refuses a face washing;
- examines each morsel of food with the intensity of a forensic investigator;
- loves something on Monday, refuses it on Tuesday and cries on Thursday because it hasn't made an appearance lately;
- insists, to the point of hysteria, on pouring the drink, unwrapping the sandwich;
- will only eat foods that are a certain temperature;
- insists on a certain bowl, even if it is unwashed;
- cries at the sight of the bottom of the bowl;
- finds one sliver of something green in the soup and refuses to eat the entire bowl.

I Wish My Kid Ate
(a List Compiled by Parents
We Know):

- Scrambled eggs, any eggs
- Sandwiches—is there an easier lunch?
- Pizza, the perfect food and always available
- Birthday cake, so she wouldn't be a social outcast at parties
- Hot dogs, then we could eat anywhere
- Grilled cheese, which can be made at anyone's house
- Macaroni and cheese, so play dates would be easier
- Vegetables, so I wouldn't feel guilty all the time
- Meat, so I wouldn't feel guilty all the time
- Anything!

ten exposures to a new food before feeling comfortable enough to even taste it. Studies indicate that most parents give up after five, but our experience has been that most parents give up after the first attempt. Making a dish ten times only for it not to be eaten ten times makes for a lot of stress and waste. However, you must try to remember the greater good and persevere. (Plus, we're advocating recipes for the whole family, so really, the worst you'll get is an extra helping for yourself!)

Maturity helps too. Around the age of six, kids may actually start eating some of the foods they have previously ignored. Of course, your one child becoming more reasonable will coincide with your next child entering the tyrant phase. All the more reason to maintain the one-meal rule (for your sanity's sake). This so-called age of reason (depending on your perspective) may be a good time to start talking about the importance of different food groups and nutrition. This should be done in a neutral environment, away from the table. They learn about the food groups in school and may even think it's fun to classify their meals into the different sections. Five- and six-year-olds are excited to learn about how their bodies function, and you might be able to work in some lessons tied to their natural interest in potty talk. They may even start choosing foods that are healthy because they understand their bodies need good fuel to keep it going.

Peer pressure can work to your benefit here. Some kids will eat things at friends' houses and daycare that they won't touch at home. Third-party endorsement is another surprisingly useful approach. Even when peer pressure fails—and we have found that with our truly picky kids, peer pressure does not work at all—you may be able to find some suitable outside influence. Start with your doctor, and if that doesn't work, try someone your kid totally admires in a way that only kids do—like a teenage cousin or a coach. And then don't be surprised when your kids eat their veggies just because Coach Mike told them to. Using other people to do your dirty work takes the pressure off the parent-child dynamic.

The urge to celebrate every time your children put something new in their mouths may be difficult to resist. Don't do it. Don't even give your partner that sly, happy look you think the kids don't understand—they do. Positive re-enforcement is still pressure. Just nod your head, smile and keep eating. You and your partner can feel smug and do your happy dance around the kitchen later.

Once a child tries something and likes it, you may be tempted to start serving it every day. Although you can increase familiarity with it by serving it a couple times a week at first, ease up and then slowly work it into the routine. If you don't, you may find yourself back where you started, with the preparation of the food you were so excited about a few weeks ago feeling like drudgery all over again.

Finally, keep in mind that there may be some foods your kids will not eat, no matter how hard you try. Bench them for now. Some things are just not worth the fight.

Exit Stage Left

Samara says the second time around she figured out the secret to feeding her kids. Now she puts the food on the table and doesn't care what they eat. This is a big change for a woman who literally put on dinner and a show—singing and dancing—all in the hopes of getting her eldest child to eat.

No More Yucky Stuff

Chapter 2
Nutrition: The Tricky Balance

We are bombarded daily by food-related images and messages: food is poison; eating the wrong thing will hurt us; it will make us fat, ugly or susceptible to serious diseases and death. On the other hand, eating the right blend of phytochemical antioxidant omegas will protect us, make us thin, beautiful and invincible.

Then we are handed a small, helpless being and told to feed it, nourish it and make it impervious to everything out there in the world. And we wonder why we're so paranoid about feeding our kids.

Medical Intervention

Rena took her son Nathan to the doctor in a panic over his diet of cereal and only cereal. The doctor looked at him, looked at her and said very calmly, "In forty years, I have never seen a child starve themselves and it won't start now."

Nutrition is only one part, albeit an important one, of what makes up a healthy child (some of the other parts being unconditional love, a safe environment and truckloads of dirt). But we need to keep things in perspective. If you are making even a half-hearted effort to ensure your kids are getting enough nutrition-wise, then they probably are. It would be pretty hard for well-meaning parents to impede the growth of a normal, healthy child. We are just trying too hard to feed these kids to actually hurt them. Even over-processed food is fortified with extra vitamins and nutrients.

If you really think your child exists on nothing but air and orange juice, take a step back and look at the big picture. For one week, write down everything your child consumes, and we mean every grape, every cracker you threw into the backseat and every sip of milk. You will be shocked to realize that your child is actually eating from more than one food group, and may even be consuming a fairly varied and healthy diet.

Now ask yourself: Do my children have lots of energy? Are they pulling me out of bed, running circles around me all day until I fall down exhausted with the TV remote in my hand? If so, then they are probably just fine.

That said, if you are really worried about your child's nutritional intake, talk to your family doctor. Don't be afraid to express your fears—many parents have the same anxieties you do. You may be surprised that after assessing your child's diet the doctor is not as alarmed as you are, and may even suggest some easy fixes to make both you and your child happy.

And while we are not nutritionists, we think the extreme focus on nutrition may be hurting as much as helping. It's important to keep a hazy idea of what your nutritional goals are: encouraging your kids to eat a variety of food groups, colours, textures and tastes. In a perfect world, every person on the planet, not to mention in your household, would eat a requisite number of servings from all the food groups every day. But in reality, they don't. Let's hope over the course of a week your kids eat fairly well, but if not, take heart—there are lots of fabulously healthy and successful people in the world who, as children, lived on white bread, processed cheese slices and powdered orange drink. You may even be one of them.

What on Earth Is a Complete Protein?

Many parents fear their children are not getting enough protein—those amino acids that make muscle tissue, blood cells, hair, nails and many other amazing things. Let us ease your minds—protein is likely the least of your troubles. Protein is everywhere, even buried in all those pure-carb treats your children love.

But that's not a *complete* protein, you say. A complete protein is one that contains all of the nine essential amino acids in specific proportions.

Meat contains complete protein, but plant-based foods lack one of the amino acids necessary to qualify as complete proteins. There are complementary foods that together make up a complete protein, like rice and beans or peanut butter and whole wheat toast. But you don't need to eat these foods together for your body to achieve a complete protein; you just need to eat the complementary components sometime that day. And even though many foods don't contain all nine amino acids, they do have *some* usable protein.

Our protein needs are less than you probably think; most North Americans eat far more than the daily requirement. Protein should make up 15 to 20 percent of your kids' daily intake (and yours too). Healthy kids need approximately .5 grams of protein per pound of body weight, or 1 gram per kilogram. That means your growing 30-pound three-year-old needs about 15 grams of protein, which can easily be found in one meal of cheese pizza and a glass of milk. Two tablespoons of peanut butter on whole wheat toast provides between 10 and 12 grams of complete protein. Even steamed veggies have 1 to 3 grams of protein per serving. So dispel the lack-of-protein fear from your mind— we're sure you can find something else to worry about.

Whose Side Are You On?

In the interest of getting a fellow soldier onside in the battle over Zachary's picky eating, Emma enlisted his pediatrician to talk to Zachary about the importance of eating a varied diet. She imagined flow charts and graphs. The pediatrician (who has a background in nutrition) went over Zachary's limited diet with him, nodded and said, "That sounds pretty good. You could try eating some more dried apricots for a little extra iron, but other than that you are doing just fine." Envisioning a lifetime of plain pasta and chicken fingers, Emma groaned inwardly, rolled her eyes— and relaxed a little.

Which Way to the
Emergency Exit?
"I actually feed myself
first, so I'm not cranky
while I feed the kids.
It's a survival thing,
like when they tell you
on the plane to put
your oxygen mask on
first, then help those
around you."
Jenna, mother of Natasha
and Alex

Rough Them up a Little

Most of us don't get enough fibre, let alone our picky kids. Anyone try-ing to toilet train a toddler knows that a lack of fibre can lead to some very uncomfortable situations. Fibre is important, not only to keep the system moving but also as a preventive measure to lower the risk of high cholesterol and heart disease.

A whole grain is a grain that has not had any of its outer layers removed. These layers act as bulk in your system, drawing water in and moving out all the, let's just say, nasty gunk. Fibre tricks the body into feeling fuller longer and may decrease your craving for fat, so teaching kids to eat lots of whole grains early means you've prepared them well for healthy arteries and hearts.

According to Health Canada, kids age one to three need 19 grams of fibre daily, and kids age three to eight need 25 grams daily. Health Canada assures us that kids eating their five servings of fruits and vegetables and five servings of whole grains daily will not have a problem meeting these targets.

How Much Fibre Is In that Food?

½ cup baked beans	7 g
1 cup whole wheat pasta	5 g
10 almonds	4 g
½ cup raspberries	4 g
½ cup peas	3.5 g
1 medium apple	3 g
1 slice whole wheat bread	2-3 g
1 medium banana	2 g

Okay, once we stop laughing hysterically at the thought of our little angels eating all those veggies, we do need to consider how to get more fibre into them. Whole grain bread is a no-brainer. But pay attention: if the label on your bag of brown bread lists wheat flour in the ingredients, throw it out—or at least don't fool yourself into thinking that it is better for you than white bread. It has to be made from *whole grain* flour or *whole wheat* flour to make a difference.

Once you start checking for fibre, you'll be surprised at how some seemingly healthy snacks, like granola bars, often have little to no fibre, while what you may consider junk food, like popcorn, is rich in fibre.

As the commercials say, fibre is your friend, and getting kids to eat whole wheat pasta, bagels and bread may not be as difficult as you thought. Generally, it's getting the adults to trade in the white stuff that's more of a problem. That said, we still embrace the use of white flour in our cookies and cakes, because life is about compromise after all.

Size Matters

You may think your kids are not eating enough because they don't eat very much at one sitting. Children's stomachs are approximately the size of their fists, and it doesn't take much to fill them up (and yet they have extraordinary stretching abilities when confronted with a large bowl of ice cream). So let the kids be the judge of when they are hungry and when they are full—it's a vital lesson to learn and, really, they are better judges than you.

Orange You Glad I Didn't Say Kale?

Why are we so hung up on vegetables? Let's be honest: most kids just don't find them as tasty, especially when compared with their close relation, fruit. There may be some adults out there who would reach for that delicious cabbage over a beautiful, fresh summertime peach—but is it realistic to expect a kid to do that?

We are all for the "five to ten servings a day" slogan. But let's remind ourselves that fruits and vegetables are in the same food group for a reason: they offer many of the same nutrients. We tend to think that all fruit has to offer is Vitamin C. But a red pepper has more Vitamin C than an orange, one cup of raspberries has more fibre than a sweet potato (and almost as much iron as spinach), and one slice of watermelon has more Vitamin A than a cup of chopped broccoli.

Fruits and vegetables add lots of vitamins and minerals to our diet, as well as fibre and phytochemicals, which act with vitamins and minerals to sustain health, strength and energy. Every colour has different benefits, so aim for the rainbow. Take your kids to the market or neighbourhood stores and let them help pick out the strangest, most colourful fruits and veggies they can find.

Every scrap of research out there says that early exposure to and eating a wide variety of fruits and veggies makes you healthier and helps protect you from a myriad of diseases. So if your kids won't eat veggies, keep serving them, keep eating them yourself and add a bowl of fruit to the dinner table. It will make you feel better.

What's the Big Diff Between Fruits and Vegetables?

The powers that be have drawn an arbitrary line between fruits and vegetables, and we seem to think it has some control over us. A fruit is the part of the plant that has the instruments of reproduction (i.e., seeds), whereas a vegetable is part of the plant itself—the leaves, stems, etc. So green pepper is a fruit, tomato is a fruit, even corn is technically a fruit, but we serve them all as vegetables. We even serve some fruits as vegetables, such as squash, but keep their cousins, melons, in the fruit category and relegate them to dessert. You can feel good about putting watermelon on the table as part of dinner now.

Milk It for What It's Worth

We have noticed that when it comes to milk, kids tend to be extremists. They either love it or won't go near it. So you may see one sibling drinking a gallon a day and another who will only ingest it if it is frozen with sprinkles on top.

Sometimes we parents encourage behaviour that we don't follow ourselves. For instance, when was the last time you had a glass of milk? If you want your kids to drink it, you're going to have to sidle up to the fridge and pour a nice cold one. (Same with veggies: studies have shown that kids tend to like the same ones their parents like, even after they have grown up. So if you don't eat that salad, can you really expect Junior to?)

Calcium is important because it helps kids grow strong bones. Toddlers require 500 milligrams a day of calcium, and young children (ages four to eight) need 800 milligrams a day. During puberty, requirements go up to over 1,000 milligrams a day.

One eight-ounce glass of milk has about 300 milligrams of calcium, plus Vitamin D, fat, protein, potassium and niacin—you've seen the ads; you know how good it is for you. So what should you give your kids if they won't drink milk? Calcium-fortified orange juice is a great invention, but some brands are sadly lacking in Vitamin D, which is an especially important nutrient for those of us who live in the Great White North, where we sometimes don't see the sun for days. Vitamin D prevents rickets, helps with calcium absorption and may do much more. Fortified soy milk is a lot sweeter than regular milk and comes in different flavours that may entice even the most reticent milk drinker.

Don't Drink This

A concerned parent is easy prey, which is why the formula makers have come out with toddler formula. We're sure that this sippy cup–friendly formula is chock full of vitamins, minerals and nutrients, and we're also sure that if confronted with a salesperson extolling its virtues, we too would be convinced it is a good idea. But unless your doctor tells you it is worth the money, we think it is a mistake to give your kids their nutrition in a cup. Teach them to eat.

This leads us to chocolate milk. Chocolate milk really is a healthy option, and we have gotten over the guilt. Chocolate milk has all the same nutrients as regular milk plus some added sugar. Since we add the syrup ourselves, we delude ourselves into believing we are not adding *that* much sugar. In this case, it's the lesser of two evils. Do what you have to do.

Don't forget, there are other calcium options—cheese, yogurt and ice cream are all good choices. The vegetables that are high in calcium are good too, but you are kidding yourself if you think any kid is going to eat enough spinach to fulfill a daily calcium requirement (but, then again, delusional thinking is a necessary part of parenting).

Strength of Iron

While some parents are haunted by the lack of fruits and vegetables in their kids' diets, others are tormented by the absence of iron. And for good reason—lack of iron is the most common nutrient deficiency in kids.

Iron helps red blood cells carry oxygen to vital organs and muscles, and without it red blood cells become pale and small, which can make you tired and reduce your brain function (kinda sounds like parenting).

Children and adults need different amounts of iron at different times in their lives, but it is especially important during growth spurts. Between the ages of one and ten your child may need 7 to 10 milligrams of iron daily. But a toddler may be more prone to iron deficiency than a preschooler because the toddler is growing at a faster rate.

Meat contains the most easily digested form of iron. Iron from plant sources, such as beans and vegetables, are harder for the body to use but become more easily absorbed when they are eaten with something containing Vitamin C, such as tomato sauce or a glass of orange juice.

If you are worried about your child's iron intake, discuss the signs of anemia (iron deficiency) with your doctor. Signs of anemia include

Vitamins A-Go-Go

There is too much conflicting evidence about vitamin supplements out there—are they a waste of money or a necessary addition to a picky eater's diet? We are opting in, hoping they are a nutritional safety net. And they come in so many flavours and shapes—even Gummy Bears! At worst, they do nothing but give us some peace of mind.

paleness, weakness, fatigue, crankiness, difficulty concentrating, frequent illnesses and intolerance of cold. But often there are no signs at all. Your doctor can do a simple blood test to determine if your child is anemic, and should be consulted before you start giving any supplements. Even a small iron deficiency should be treated.

Fat Is Good

Everything tastes better with fat. You could fry this page in bacon fat and we would probably eat it. For kids, that's okay, because their bodies need fat to grow.

A child's most basic need for growth is calories, and fat is packed with calories in a very efficient way. Their first food—breast milk—is 50 percent fat and it is, by design, the perfect way to start.

The Canadian Paediatric Society doesn't have any hard and fast rules about fat intake for children. In a position paper sent out to pediatricians and available on its website, the society states that "during the preschool and childhood years, nutritious food choices should not be eliminated or restricted because of fat content." It recommends that children under the age of two have a high-fat diet and that early childhood be considered a transition period aiming toward a diet that is approximately 30 percent fat by the teenage years. A low-fat diet is not advised for children, as they may not get enough calories for their growing needs. (If only that were true for those of us standing around the playground with a few pounds to lose.)

What *is* a concern is the type of fat that is consumed. Saturated fats, which come from animal-derived foods (meat, milk, poultry and butter) and some plants (coconut and palm), should only make up 10 percent of anyone's diet. Saturated fat raises LDL (low-density lipoprotein), the bad cholesterol. But the real problem is trans fatty acids. Trans fats are made by taking unsaturated fat and throwing hydrogen at it (look for hydrogenated fat in ingredients labels). Widely practised within the

Iron Will Needed

Here are some good ways to get iron into a child's diet. Plant sources of iron are best absorbed when taken with Vitamin C, and some even say with white wine (only for the grown-ups, of course). Consult your doctor before adding any medicinal iron supplements to your child's diet.

- Fortified cereals and oatmeal, especially when served with fruit.
- Dried fruit and pumpkin seeds (which some kids even consider a treat!).
- Molasses and wheat germ (use it as an excuse to bake).
- Liverwurst on a cracker.
- Eggs.

Liam, age three, who was standing in one spot, turned to his mother, Natalie, and said, "Look, I'm food." Then he started running around and said, "Look, I'm fast food!"

processed foods industries, this procedure stabilizes the fat, allowing the processed food to last for a long, long time. While a good choice for them, it's a bad choice for you because it can lower HDL (high-density lipoprotein), the good cholesterol, and the possible long-term effects of that can lead to heart disease. Public pressure is forcing many companies to remove trans fats from their products, but until all food is trans fat–free, buy other, healthier items.

The good choices are unsaturated fats, which are found in canola, safflower and olive oils, avocados, nuts and seeds. These help lower LDL and are the ones you should stock up on. And while we're not about to give up butter, we do suggest you make a conscious effort to use the healthier fats wherever possible. Repeat after us: Fat is good, fat is healthy. You may have to reprogram yourself. As long as your children are given a wide variety of healthy foods, fat should not be an issue. Sadly, our need for a high-fat diet dwindles with age.

No Reading Obscure Nutrition Studies!

Every day, it seems there is another nutrition article to strike fear in our hearts. At the risk of oversimplifying the nutrition issue, we try to shake off our anxieties and be optimistic that our kids are getting what they need from food and that vitamin supplements are filling in the gaps. We stock our kitchens with a healthy selection of food choices. We cut up tons of fruit, try to cook the most delicious healthy food possible and remember to sit down and enjoy it ourselves. But ultimately it is up to our children to decide whether they will join us or not. This is all about a lot more than iron or fibre content. It's about teaching your children to make life choices. And besides, life would be no fun if all our food were taken as one big freeze-dried supplement.

Quick Reminder

Just in case you forgot your primary school lessons, the basic food groups are:

- five to twelve servings of bread and grain;
- five to ten servings of fruit and vegetables;
- two to four servings of dairy;
- two to four servings of meat and meat alternatives;
- and the bonus group of fats, oils and sweets, which are to be used in moderation.

In Hindsight

In 1961, Canada's Food Guide suggested two servings of bread or grains with butter or margarine; three vegetable servings, one of them being potatoes; and two servings of fruit, including juice. And despite what we would consider today to be some unhealthy directions, things turned out okay!

I ATE IT ALL

Chapter 3
The First Year:
After This, It's All Downhill

This is it. Food. You have the high chair and the bibs, the floor is covered with a tarp, and you have lots of colour-coordinated plastic bowls and spoons. Now what?

Take a deep breath. Feeding babies is fun. They make big messes and lots of funny faces, and they really love their food. The first few months on solids are all about teaching your baby to experience tastes and textures and the wonders of food.

Dress for the Occasion

You will soon realize that your baby's shirt has had a more nutritious meal than its wearer, but don't stop to wonder about the long-term effects of squash on eardrums—clean that shirt! Immediate action is required! Throw the offending garment into the kitchen sink with dish soap if you have to. Or keep some stain remover in the kitchen and rub it in pronto. Stain sticks are also handy— keep one by the dirty laundry hamper, so you can rub it in and forget about it.

And every seasoned parent knows: you must use an oxygen-based stain remover.

As for the baby, nothing less than a decontamination hose-down will do.

We feel that giving your baby a wide range of foods in the beginning will pay off in the end. There is no magic formula for producing a good eater, but creating a stress-free environment and giving your baby delicious and healthy options are good habits to cultivate early—both for your child and for you. If you were able to breastfeed your baby, then you may have started them into the world of interesting flavour. Breast milk tastes different according to what the mother is eating—so your varied diet has been influencing your baby's palate. (Studies have also shown that when a nursing mother eats garlic an hour or so before a feed, the baby feeds longer and gets more milk—so there's another great reason to eat good-for-you garlic.)

In hindsight, our friends (okay, us too) will admit that perhaps they were a little too structured when it came to their first baby's eating habits. As we watch child number two (and we won't even tell you about the travesty of number three) munch on bakery muffins or chicken nuggets and wash it all down with a great big glass of juice, we remind ourselves that food is good for our babies. You cannot control everything they put into their mouths, and besides, you shouldn't even try. If you do, you will definitely have a picky eater on your hands. And we will bet you the price of the book on that one.

There are lots of resources available with detailed information about how, what and when to feed your baby (see Resources on page 204). In this chapter, we've included the basic methods for preparing baby food, along with some suggestions of good starter foods that are delicious, easy to prepare and will set your baby up for a lifetime of good eating.

Parents get caught up in what colours to start with and it which order. But really, it's hard to go wrong. It doesn't really matter if you start with orange foods, white foods or green foods. Enjoy these first few months—food-wise, it's all downhill from here.

Four to Six Months—Matchless Mushes

Most doctors and the Canadian Paediatric Society now recommend waiting until six months of age before starting solids. Don't rush into feedings because you believe your mother when she tells you that solids will help your baby sleep through the night. It's just another item on the long list of old wives' tales that plague parenting. Your mom, grandmother, aunt or nanny may have made the hole bigger in your bottle and watered down some rice cereal for you to drink, but here in North America that's now considered force-feeding and is a big no-no! In fact, as babies learn to digest new forms of food, they may even wake up a little more often.

On the other hand, don't regard the six months date as the magical age to start solids. Watch your baby, not the calendar. Your baby may be ready sooner, especially if there are older siblings around to mimic. If you suspect yours might be ready to start, ask your doctor for advice but, ultimately, trust your instincts.

Watch for signs that your baby is ready for food, like that hungry-desperate look that appears while watching you put food into your mouth, not unlike how you would imagine a lion watching a herd of antelopes. Some babies even mimic chewing motions and bring a spoon up to their mouths (although more likely up to their noses). And don't worry if those tiny fingers grab a roll off your plate a week short of the pre-scribed six-month waiting period—Baby is trying to tell you something.

The first time you give your baby some food, they may push it out with their tongue as soon as it enters their mouth. This is the natural extrusion reflex, useful for breastfeeding, but, as you have noticed, a bit counterproductive for eating. Be patient; it may take a week or so, but they will learn how to get that food down.

The good news is that if you have waited until six months to feed your baby solids, then there are no hard and fast rules about what food to start with and what order in which to give it. Baby's body is ready for

A Good Start

When Max, Eshun's first child, was just five months old, he showed he was ready for solids by swiping a wedge of watermelon from his father's plate. He had a great time mimicking his father eating it and watching Dad's reactions as he took each bite. It made for a wonderful photo opportunity and showed his parents that he was more than ready to start solid foods. Needless to say, the bland rice cereal he was offered later that same week was soundly rejected, and Eshun became convinced that Max was going to live on watermelon for the rest of his life (instead, it's been chicken fingers and burnt toast).

food, pretty much any food. And we really mean any food, so don't worry about feeding the "wrong thing."

In fact, if you start doing research on this topic, your head will soon be spinning because every single book, website and resource will tell you something different. And since the experts can't conclusively decide at how many months of age kiwi or lentils should be served, we are going to ignore them and make the decision based on our babies' reactions.

Across cultures, you'd be amazed at what babies are eating at a given age. All over the world, Baby gets what everyone else is eating, including rice, beans and even curry—there often isn't enough time or money or access to variety to start planning alternative menus.

In North America, cereal is usually the suggested first food because it is bland, has a high iron content and can be mixed with breast milk or formula for a familiar taste. Rice cereal is recommended first because it has the lowest rate of allergies, but watch out—there may be constipation in your future. Most babies prefer oatmeal as it tastes a lot better, and it won't stop them up as much. It takes about a week to figure out the whole swallowing thing; after that, get ready to cart around little containers of brightly coloured mash wherever you go. You may find that your little one prefers the veggies and fruits to that bland cereal, but the iron is good for them, so mix it all together.

Start with your chosen fruit or vegetable. Add a new one every couple of days. Sometimes it can take ten exposures to get a child (no matter what age) used to a new food, so don't get discouraged if the peas come flying out on the first few attempts.

Disclaimer: Once again, we feel the need to remind you that we are not nutritionists. We are mothers trying to survive in a chaotic world. If you are really concerned about what foods to feed your baby in which month, there are lots of books, websites and other resources out there. But we are sticking to our theory that it doesn't really matter if peas come before or after bananas.

Guilt, Fried

Zachary had just started finger food when, one evening, he reached over and grabbed a french fry from his father Micah's plate. Emma was ridden with guilt—the fat, the salt. When she admitted the transgression to her mothers' group, the leader (a mother of three) laughed and said that french fries are a perfect baby food—great size, soft in the middle and salty. Don't start feeling guilty now; you've got a long way to go, she said. And she was right!

Making homemade baby food is ridiculously easy and tastes a lot better than the stuff that comes in jars. But it does take some planning and can seem daunting in the face of all our other obligations, so we always have a store of jars in the cupboard too. There are lots of good-quality jarred foods available. There are also a few lines of frozen baby foods. Your best bet is the organic varieties; read the labels closely to avoid filler ingredients and added sweeteners.

The great thing about making your baby's food yourself is that it forces you to have lots of fruits and vegetables around, and you find yourself eating more of the healthy stuff too.

Baby food companies don't do anything special to a banana, so buying a jar of mushable food is a total waste of money. But other foods need a few minutes of TLC in the kitchen. Steaming, roasting and even sautéing are our favourite ways to make baby food. They are fast and easy. And best of all, by not immersing the vegetables in water, you aren't washing away all the healthy nutrients. And when your baby's in the mush stage, please don't forget delicious lentils. They are 25 percent protein, rich in iron and Vitamin B and tasty. Teach your baby to love them with the starter form of red lentils, which turn into a vibrant mush. Brown lentils keep their form when cooked and are great for babies making the move towards finger food.

We are not total gear-heads, but there are some tools that we like to have on hand to make baby food. Most of these items will sit unused and cause clutter once Baby moves on to "people food." At the least expensive end, you can buy small, hand-cranked baby food grinders, which use your strength to squish food through tiny holes. They are quick, easy to use and indispensable. Or you could purchase a food mill, which is just a large version of the baby grinder. They're more expensive but may have a longer shelf life, as they make great mashed potatoes for the whole family. And a mini food processor or blender is a big investment, but they do chop huge loads of stuff quickly and are really the only effective way to make smooth purées

Portion Control

Baby food jars are a random size. It does not matter if a baby eats half a jar, a whole jar or two entire jars. It is important to have faith that Baby knows the difference between being satisfied and still being hungry. We will guarantee that he knows better than you and he should be allowed to eat as much as he wants. In fact, most adults could learn from babies about how to listen to their bodies for signs of fullness and hunger. We could certainly use some retraining on that!

Brightly Coloured Things

Once Baby starts eating more solid foods, you may notice some differences *down there* in the diaper area. Many parents have gone to the doctor worried about orange poo, only to learn that an overabundance of carrots or sweet potatoes was the culprit. And it just keeps getting better—wait till you see what peas can do.

from stringy things like green beans. Of course, a fork and a potato masher are also extremely handy in a crunch.

Once you have squished, pulverized or mashed up the food, freeze it in ice cube trays. You can even layer different foods in one cube (baked sweet potato and apple for instance). Once frozen, pop the cubes into a resealable plastic bag, and don't forget to label it. Serve one or two cubes for a quick meal. If you're reheating by microwave, remember to mix well to avoid hot spots.

Ready to Go

These foods are baby food—ready and as close to baby take-out food as you can get. Just mash and go.

- Avocado
- Banana
- Ripe peaches, plums, apricots, pears, blueberries
- Mango, papaya
- Tofu
- Yogurt
- Cottage cheese
- Canned beans (kidney, pinto, etc.)

Steaming

Steaming is a wonderful way to cook harder fruits and vegetables before you purée them. You can purchase pots that have a perforated layer, or an inexpensive collapsible steamer insert which will fit in almost any pot. But please make sure you put enough water in the bottom of the pot. We have both made the mistake of letting the water run out and ended up with burnt cookware and inedible food.

- Apples
- Asparagus
- Bok choy
- Broccoli
- Carrots
- Cauliflower
- Zucchini and summer squash
- Peas
- Green beans

Spoon-feeding

Sometimes watching our babies learn to eat with a spoon is just too aggravating. Our sense of control takes over as we efficiently spoon the mush into their waiting mouths. Elizabeth got over her need for neatness by putting eleven-month-old Theo in the high chair, then handing him a spoon and some food. She would tell him it was his turn to feed himself because Mommy was busy. She then focused on making dinner, not on the complete mess that was going on behind her. After a while, Theo figured out how to do it.

Sautéing

To sauté, you cook the fruit or vegetable in a little fat over high heat until soft and then you purée. Adding fat essentially adds flavour. And since kids are supposed to have a high-fat diet until the age of two, it's no problem to use good fats such as olive oil or canola regularly. Butter, used sparingly, makes everything taste that much better. And once you think your baby is ready, add a pinch of minced garlic, cumin or cinnamon to the pan.

- Apples
- Red and green peppers
- Leafy greens, such as spinach
- Zucchini and summer squash

Roasting

Easily our favourite method of preparation, roasting reduces the liquid content, intensifies the flavours of fruits and vegetables, and caramelizes the natural sugars along the way. Cut these into chunks, throw them in the oven at 400°F and let them caramelize in their skins. Don't forget to make enough for yourself. You may need to add a bit of liquid (water, stock, juice, breast milk, etc.) in order to purée.

- Sweet potatoes
- Pears
- Winter squash (butternut, acorn, etc.)
- Apples
- Turnips
- Stone fruit (peaches, plums, etc.)

And I'll Have the Smushed Plums with a Side of Mushy Peas

We try to live by an important rule: Never feed your baby something you wouldn't eat yourself. Which means, yes, you should taste everything, even if the thought of those brownish mushy peas makes you a bit nauseous. Tanya forced herself to do a taste test of chicken purées. She still wonders what they did to the jarred food to make it so nasty that it left a coating on the roof of her mouth. She resolved that if she couldn't even swallow it, then she couldn't really feed it to her baby with a clear conscience.

Seven to Eight Months—Totally Texture

Now it's time to start branching out—especially when it comes to texture. You don't want to end up with an older baby who eats only mush at birthday number one. Your baby doesn't need teeth to eat chunks. Those gums will do the job just fine.

Yogurt, cottage cheese and soft tofu are baby favourites and are all great mixed into your purées. If you are making your own baby food, start trying to make it a little bit thicker and lumpier. Small noodles, such as stars, orzo and pastina, boiled in chicken or veggie stock, will soon be a staple (and make an excellent lunch for you too).

We think meat should be introduced at around eight or nine months. We do not have any scientific reason for this; we just think putting meat in the blender is gross. So we wait until Baby can handle a chunkier texture such as ground meat or can pick up small pieces of tender chicken or stewed beef. Chicken legs (with the pin bone removed) and pork ribs are very tender and can keep Baby busy for an entire meal. Soups made from poultry or meat stock can be started with the other first foods at six months.

Baby is starting to get the gist of the whole feeding thing and may be grabbing the spoon from you. We know you'd prefer not to let Junior make a mess, but you have to. And we're not joking. It's very important that your child develop a sense of independence and feel a measure of control. And this means a mess, and we mean a big one. Babies will play with their food and squish it between their fingers; they will rub it on their faces and get it in their ears. Messes can be cleaned up; a negative attitude about mealtime can last a lifetime. Your baby will probably enjoy having a spoon to play with, draw with and drop on the floor, over and over again.

The high chair should be positioned beside you at the dinner table so that Baby is enjoying mealtime along with you. Babies are little mimics and will learn what to do from watching you eat your dinner.

Here Comes the Milk

At the age of one, kids should be weaned off formula and on to homogenized milk. By this age, they should be getting most of their nutrition from food, and since formula is so filling, they may not be eating properly. When kids turn two, homogenized milk should be replaced with 1 or 2 percent milk because of the fat content. This can be done by mixing the two milks and decreasing the amount of whole milk at each bottle. You could put them on skim, but it tastes like water, and the fat in 1 or 2 percent milk is good for them. (Besides, fuller-fat milk tastes better in Mommy's coffee.)

Warning! Kids, even babies, have personal likes and dislikes and they will (gasp!) be different than yours. If your baby spits out something again and again (remember that it can take ten times to "normalize" a food), that may indicate an actual dislike of the texture or the taste. So if after many exposures Baby continues to dislike avocado, even if *you* think it is heavenly, then accept it—you never know what the future may hold.

Nine to Twelve Months—Finger Foods

The transition to finger foods can be smooth or chunky (ha ha). Baby should be pretty adept at eating fruit and veggie mush, and may even be a bit bored by it. It's time to widen the culinary world with chunkier textures and more table food.

Around nine months, watch for Baby to develop the pincer grasp—the ability to use the thumb and index finger to pick up small pieces. That means it's time for finger foods.

Alongside the dependable mush, place small pieces of food on the tray for Baby to pick up. If mashed carrots are a favourite, place a few pieces of cooked carrots beside the bowl. Most will end up on the floor, but that's okay. Take a deep breath, count to ten and clean it up later. It's only food on the floor.

Object permanence is a big lesson at this time of life. Babies are trying to figure out if things disappear when they can't see them, and one of the ways they learn this is by throwing food on the floor, again and again and again. It does not necessarily mean they are done, nor does it mean they hate the food. It is extremely tiresome for you, but this fun game will dominate mealtime for a while.

Now is also the time to introduce table foods. Most of the food you and your family eat can be mashed or cut up in small pieces for Baby. Some things may need to be moistened with stock, water or formula, but

Every Phase Has Its Challenges!

When we met our book agent, Hilary (mom of two little ones), she was terribly frustrated that Cameron (then one) was constantly throwing his food off his high chair. "It was driving me crazy to see whatever fabulous thing was on the menu that night (okay, peas don't involve much effort) go flying off in every direction. We tried everything to get him to stop, but nothing worked. I remember one day, when I was at the end of my rope, picking up a piece of pasta myself and flinging it at the wall. It actually made me feel better, although I'm sure it isn't endorsed in any parenting manuals. Other grown-ups assured me that Cameron would grow out of it, and sure enough, he did."

Baby will be pleased to be eating the same thing as you. This is no small landmark; it lays the groundwork for enjoying family meals later on.

Unfortunately, this is often the stage when nervous parents look around for baby food books to start preparing special menus for Junior. We think that this could be the source of all evil (okay, not all) when it comes to picky eating. Your baby does NOT need to eat a special meal of chicken, rice and beans while you all eat pizza. If you create special, intricate "toddler-friendly" meals for your child, gauge your reaction when the food you slaved over is rejected. Are you feeling resentful? Are you putting on the pressure? If so, you could be setting yourself up for a lifetime of pickiness. (Don't say we didn't warn you.) And think about this: If you want to prepare a special meal, shouldn't your whole family be able enjoy the result? Here's a challenge: Take your eleven-month-old to a restaurant, any ethnicity or price level. There should be at least one thing on the menu for your baby to eat—soup, rice, grilled cheese. If you cannot find one thing, then you have already sheltered your child too much from the joys of real food.

Once they have that pincer grasp, try these finger-friendly goodies.

- Melon—cantaloupe, honeydew, watermelon
- Mango
- Fresh or frozen blueberries
- Cooked asparagus spears
- Cooked lentils
- Canned kidney beans, sliced in half lengthwise
- Soft cheese, grated or cut into small cubes
- Chunky cereal
- Ladyfinger cookies
- Pieces of toast with creamed cottage cheese
- Small cubes of medium-firm tofu
- Pieces of pancake
- Egg yolk omelet
- Pieces of veggies, meat and beans from soup

Heimlich, Anyone?

There is a difference between choking and gagging. Gagging is good; choking is bad. If your child really is choking, you will know—there will not be any breathing sounds. Call 911.

Babies have a more sensitive gag reflex than adults, so don't freak out if they gag. If they are gagging, they are learning when to swallow pieces and when not to. Give them something to drink and let them try again if they want. And then try again in a few days. Remember, they've only swallowed liquid and mush before now.

Foods that are round, very slippery or extremely hard should be avoided or cut up. These include hot dogs, grapes, popcorn, nuts, gum, raisins, marshmallows and gummy treats.

Tip: Coating slippery pieces in "cracker dust" (crushed- up Cheerios or graham crackers) may give Baby a firmer grasp.

I Can Do It

Emma's precocious youngest, Talia, rejected mush at nine months and wanted to feed herself. Her daily diet consisted of over-cooked broccoli, chunks of sweet potato, tofu and blueberries, all of which made it into her mouth with varying accuracy.

Tofu Triumph

Kris earns our respect, not only because she has three boys under three, but because she manages to find the energy to feed them healthily and with a sense of humour. She has some tricks up her sleeve: one dinner is tofu straight from the package and another is steamed fillets of sole with veggies. Kids who eat tofu and fish—it *can* happen.

- Tofu scrambler (a substitute for scrambled eggs, found at health food stores)
- Homemade gelatin treats (page 173)
- Small pieces of pasta boiled in stock, or small, cooked pasta mixed with cheese
- French fries (hey, *you're* eating them)

Waiting List

There are some foods that should be introduced slowly because of their potential to cause allergies. Unfortunately some of the information can be quite confusing. If you or your partner comes from an especially allergic family, consult with your doctor before introducing any potential allergens. While other foods can be introduced as you wish, this guide may help you decide when to introduce these foods:

- Wheat: Wheat cereals and products should be started after all other grains have been introduced. If your baby has not reacted to grains such as oatmeal and barley, the likelihood of a wheat allergy is very low. But the general recommendation is to not start babies on wheat products until after seven months. The good news is that once babies can eat baked products, the heel of the bread or toast strips can keep them busy for ages while you finish your own meal.
- Citrus fruits/strawberries/tomatoes: These foods are more likely than others to cause allergic reactions and should not be given until about eight months.
- Eggs: Eggs are another food that makes it difficult to be a parent. Egg yolks are very nutritious and easy for babies to swallow (and parents to prepare), but exposure to egg whites before about twelve months old can lead to an

allergy. Generally, baked goods made with whole eggs are just fine.

- Milk: Milk should never be given in a bottle or cup before Baby's first birthday—breast milk or formula is the first choice. But yogurt, soft grated cheese and cottage cheese are delicious and healthy foods for Baby at about seven months.
- Honey: Honey can contain a potentially harmful bacteria that causes botulism and can be dangerous to babies under one year. And by the way, honey is not any more nutritious than sugar, so your baby is not missing much.
- Shellfish: Shellfish is one of the potentially scary ones and should be introduced only after one year.
- Nuts: There is a lot of fear about introducing nuts into a child's diet. On one hand, nuts are extremely nutritious and easy, and most kids like them (especially smeared on bread with lots of jam). But on the other, they can be very dangerous to some kids, especially those who have an anaphylactic reaction to them. Giving foods containing nuts to your child can be a highly stressful event. If there is a history of peanut or tree nut allergy in your family, you may want to talk to your doctor about doing an allergy test after one year of age in the safety of the doctor's office. (Smearing a smidge of peanut butter on your child's cheek does not count as an allergy test.) Wait until at least eighteen months for tree nuts (almonds, hazelnuts, walnuts, pecans) and up to the age of three for peanuts. But don't wait so long that you live in fear of nuts in public places or so you miss the chance to turn your child on to a tasty and convenient source of protein.

What Is Anaphylaxis?

Anaphylaxis is a serious, possibly life-threatening allergic reaction. The most common food allergens are peanuts, tree nuts, seafood, egg and milk products.

According to Anaphylaxis Canada, approximately 1 to 2 percent of Canadians live with the risk of an ana-phylactic reaction.

During an anaphylactic reaction, the body releases a tremendous amount of histamine, causing the throat to tighten. Some of the symptoms to watch for are: tingling, itchy or puffy lips, tongue and/or throat; hoarse-ness; hives; nausea and vomiting; tightening of the throat and difficult breathing.

Call 911 if your child has trouble breathing or speaking, develops a swollen tongue, becomes confused or loses consciousness while eating.

Happy Birthday to You!

By one year, the transition to adult food should be complete. If you have been congratulating yourself on your child's good eating habits, here's a warning: it ain't over yet. Many children cut back on how much they eat after their first birthday; their growth rate slows and so does their appetite. Your anxiety may grow in proportion to their declining appetites, but take heart—it's perfectly normal for kids to get choosier and eat smaller portions as they get older.

After your child's first birthday, collect all remaining jars of baby food and give them to your local food bank. It is time to move on. Be excited—now your job is to make family meals that an entire family can enjoy together. These meals can be kid-friendly, and we have lots of ideas on how to do that, without falling into patterns that will be near impossible to break. Keep reading.

Sugar So Sweet

You have probably diligently avoided sugar and all things chocolate for your child during the first year. Aside from the hypocrisy of scarfing down Timbits at your mothers' group while poor Junior gets a sugar-free carrot muffin, it's time to reassess your fear of sugar. Denying babies sugar in the first year will not mean they won't develop a taste for it—kids can sniff out sugar like dogs looking for a bone, and will love it from the very first moment it hits their tiny tongues. If sugar becomes a forbidden food, expect to find bags of treats under their pillows as soon as they figure out how to sneak it into the house. So put some sugar in the birthday cake. If you don't, no one will enjoy it. And wouldn't that be sad?

Don't
Rush Me,
I'm
Eating

Chapter 4
Breakfast: Your Best Chance to Stuff Them Full of Health

Kids wake up hungry. Their bodies did a lot of hard work overnight, and they need to replenish their fuel tanks.

We don't really need to repeat the line about breakfast being the most important meal of the day, do we? You've heard it before. You know that kids who eat breakfast concentrate better, have more energy and are generally nicer to be around. So run, or sleepwalk, to the kitchen and give them something delicious and nutritious, or they could end up being the kids who sleep through math class.

Setting a good example is key. Do *you* eat breakfast? By this we mean, do you actually sit down and eat food that does not drip out of the coffee maker? You cannot expect your kids to understand the importance of breakfast if you don't bother with it. We know you don't really feel like eating before 11 a.m., but having breakfast will grow on you, and eventually you'll wonder how you functioned without it. Breakfast is a particularly good chance to get those picky eaters eating something healthy, because despite the chaos, everyone really does love some kind of breakfast food.

Day In, Day Out

Many kids eat the same thing each and every day for breakfast and are perfectly happy and healthy. Eshun's kids eat toast—toast with peanut butter and jam or honey, or Rory's favourite—peanut butter and "chock-lick," the chocolaty European treat, Nutella.

Just Say No

Sugar cereals are no better than candy and should be banned from your house (except on special occasions). We use our unequivocal ban on sugar cereals as an opener to talk about the power of marketing and commercials with our kids. Even preschoolers understand when someone is trying to sell them something.

Experts say that a healthy breakfast combines three of the five food groups and should contain approximately 25 percent of your daily nutrition requirements. This is actually far less complicated than it sounds. A steaming bowl of oatmeal with milk and a few pieces of fruit does the trick. Or how about a tortilla roll-up with turkey, cheese and grated apple? Yogurt hits both the dairy and the protein requirements.

Protein is a crucial part of breakfast but often forgotten. Ever wonder why a bowl of cereal with a bit of milk leaves you famished by 10 a.m.? That's because those carbs burn off very quickly, whereas protein takes longer to digest and will keep you going longer.

There's just something fun about breakfast food, and it should be spread around a little. More than one family eats pancakes for dinner and oatmeal at snack time.

Here are a few more creative, on-the-go breakfasts.

- Oatcakes with creamed cottage cheese and jam.
- Toast with cheese and pear slices.
- Rice cakes with tahini and honey.
- Yogurt with granola and a glass of juice.
- Whole wheat pita with smoked salmon and cream cheese.
- Dry cereal in a cup with a handful of berries.
- Eggs—hard-boiled the day before.
- Breakfast burritos—leftovers with or without cheese rolled up in a tortilla and warmed through.

We're trying to inspire you to face the morning by providing some recipes that are good for weekdays as well as ones for leisurely weekends. So make breakfast mandatory for you and your loved ones: everyone will be happier and healthier, and your morning will be less chaotic—okay, not really . . .

Banana French Toast

In some kind of rebellion against his heritage, Zachary will not eat French toast made from challah (egg bread). He only likes it if it's made from a baguette, so this version of French toast is a new favourite in Emma's house. Our recipe includes a serving of fruit which naturally sweetens the French toast, so you can try to get your kids to ease up on the maple syrup (ha ha).

Of course, feel free to experiment with other kinds of bread—but you need one with an open, holey texture, or the bananas will just sit on the surface and stick to your pan.

4	eggs
1 cup	milk
1 tsp	cinnamon
Pinch	salt
2	ripe bananas, mashed
1	baguette (preferably day-old), cut into ¾-inch slices
3 tbsp	butter
	Icing sugar and maple syrup (optional)

Combine eggs, milk, cinnamon and salt in a large bowl; whisk to combine. Stir in mashed banana.

Add baguette slices to egg mixture in batches. Use a fork to squish the bread and soften the crust so the bread soaks up the mixture.

Melt butter in a nonstick frying pan over medium heat. Add as many baguette slices as will fit; fry for about 2 minutes per side or until slices are golden. Serve immediately, either plain, dusted with icing sugar or drizzled with maple syrup.

Makes 4 servings.

Tip: Emma's husband has fond childhood memories of a French toast grilled cheese sandwich, which is easily made with these same ingredients (minus the banana and cinnamon). Place thin slices of cheese, such as Cheddar or mozzarella, between two slices of bread. Dip the sandwich in the egg-milk mixture, turning to soak well. Place in pan over medium heat, pressing the sandwich with a spatula until the cheese is melted, and then flip it over to cook the other side.

Buttermilk Pancakes

Tip: We usually add some form of fruit to the batter—a large banana, mashed, or a finely grated apple is a great addition, as are fresh or frozen berries. As an eight-year-old, Eshun always chose chocolate chips—maybe you could save this for a very special treat.

Eshun has been the family pancake maker since she was about eight years old, and has tried more than your average number of pancake recipes. This one is the best, but we can't claim it for our own. It is essentially Marion Cunningham's recipe, which we found in a bread book by Peter Reinhart called *Crust and Crumb*. We tinkered with it a little, but you be the judge. We may finally wean Emma's family off pancake mix for good. This recipe makes a ton of pancakes and is THE reason we always have buttermilk in the refrigerator. Leftovers can be reheated in the toaster oven.

1 ⅓ cups	all-purpose flour
⅔ cup	whole wheat flour
1 tsp	baking soda
½ tsp	salt
2	large eggs
2 cups	buttermilk
¼ cup	butter, melted
	Butter or vegetable oil for cooking

Combine flours, baking soda and salt in a large bowl; stir with a fork to blend.

Crack eggs into flour mixture. Pour buttermilk over eggs. Using a fork, stir ingredients until a lumpy batter forms and all flour is absorbed; do not overmix. Mix in melted butter.

Swirl a little butter or vegetable oil over the surface of an electric griddle or a large frying pan over medium heat. Using $1/4$-cup measuring cup, pour several dollops of batter into the pan.

When bubbles begin to appear on tops of the pancakes, flip them over and continue cooking for about 1 minute or until browned on both sides and tender in the middle.

Makes 4 servings, or 18 medium-size pancakes.

Mix Magic

If you really can't get out of the pancake mix routine, make your own! Double the dry ingredients and mix well. It will last for months and months in an airtight container.

Then to one cup of the mixture, add one egg, one cup of buttermilk and two tablespoons of butter. The results may not be quite as perfect as making the whole recipe, but do you want perfect or do you want fast?

Multi-grain Buttermilk Waffles

Whole wheat flour doesn't usually add anything to a recipe taste-wise, but we continue to use it because we know it's good for us. But the waffle iron toasts the whole wheat somewhat so that it actually adds a little *je ne sais quoi* along with the crunch of cornmeal to make it a truly delicious, healthy breakfast. These can be made on a leisurely weekend morning, and then leftovers can be toasted for a fast weekday treat.

Tip: When combining dry ingredients, it is best to stir with a fork or whisk to make sure all the ingredients are thoroughly mixed.

1 cup	all-purpose flour
⅓ cup	whole wheat flour
¼ cup	cornmeal
1 tsp	baking soda
1 tsp	baking powder
1 tsp	salt
¼ tsp	cinnamon
2	large eggs
1 ½ cups	buttermilk
2 tbsp	brown sugar
2 tbsp	vegetable oil

Combine flours, cornmeal, baking soda, baking powder, salt and cinnamon in a large bowl; stir with a fork to blend.

Crack eggs into centre of flour mixture. Pour buttermilk, brown sugar and oil over eggs. Stir ingredients with a fork until lumpy batter forms. Do not overmix. Let sit for 5 minutes while waffle iron heats up.

Lightly grease a heated waffle iron.

Using about 1/3 cup of the batter per waffle, cook for about 2 minutes or until crisp and golden. You may need to regrease the waffle iron between waffles. Serve immediately; or cool on a rack and wrap in plastic to reheat and serve later.

Makes 10 medium-size waffles.

Waffle Irons

Waffles seem more special than pancakes. It must be because you need to use a piece of equipment that is big, heavy and totally useless for any other application. Eshun has had a succession of fantastic waffle irons she has picked up at garage sales, and she swears the older the better.

Mushroom and Spinach Frittata

Easier than an omelette, faster than a quiche—it's a frittata. We make frittatas for breakfast, brunch and even an emergency dinner. Granted, it's not a Monday morning, rush-out-the-door kind of thing. Use this recipe as a guideline and vary the filling ingredients according to what's in your refrigerator. Push the vegetables away from one section of the pan to make a plain "piece" if you don't think the kids are up to picking out the things they don't like. This is even a good place to hide some left-over cooked vegetables from last night's dinner.

5	large eggs
2 tbsp	cream or milk
	Salt and freshly ground pepper
2 tbsp	olive oil
1 cup	chopped onion
1 cup	chopped green pepper
1 cup	chopped mushrooms (white or brown)
2 cups	baby spinach
1 tbsp	chopped fresh coriander or flat-leaf parsley
$\frac{1}{2}$ cup	grated Cheddar cheese

Scrambled Eggs

If we could build a time machine and warp speed back a few years, we would get our kids to eat scrambled eggs. They are full of protein and iron and can be whipped up quickly (if only the pan could be cleaned as fast), and lots of things like cheese and veggies can be thrown in. *Our* kids, of course, get all weird around them, as if they were live worms. But if we had desensitized them early . . .

Preheat broiler to high.

Combine eggs and cream in a small bowl; beat with a whisk until uniformly mixed. Season well with salt and pepper.

Heat oil in an 8-inch, ovenproof nonstick frying pan over medium-low heat. Add onions; cook for 5 minutes or until soft and lightly golden. Add green peppers; sauté for 2 minutes or until softened. Add mushrooms; cook for 2 minutes or until juices release. Season with salt and pepper to taste. Stir in spinach; cook for 1 minute or until just beginning to wilt.

Pour egg mixture into pan, stirring to distribute vegetables evenly. Sprinkle coriander and cheese over top; use a spoon to submerge them slightly in egg mixture.

Cook for 2 minutes or until eggs have set on the bottom and around the edges of the pan. Place the pan in the oven and broil for 2 minutes or until eggs are fully set and top is golden.

Makes 4 servings.

He's So Frontal

Emma's best friend is a pediatric neurologist (and a perfectly normal person), and while she generally separates her medical training from her mothering, sometimes it creeps in. For instance, she was watching two-year-old Theo obsess about the size and shape of his chicken finger when she uttered in exasperation, "He's so frontal!" She then explained that the frontal lobes of the brain don't fully develop until the early 20s, but they are the part of the brain that help you prioritize, problem solve and generally act like a valuable member of society. This means it's totally normal for your child to fall apart if the drinking straw is the wrong colour.

Oatmeal for the Week

In a Flap over Flax

Do you ever pass by ground flaxseed, natural bran or wheat germ at the supermarket and wonder what to do with them? We do. But when we do pick them up and remember to sprinkle them into our granola, smoothies or oatmeal, we feel like the best mothers on earth. We have added fibre! Omega-3 fatty acids! Iron and Vitamin E! They are so easy to hide, so why do we leave the half-empty bags at the back of the refrigerator waiting for the next health craze? Be better than us and sneak healthy fibre in wherever you can.

There is something very comforting about a steaming bowl of oatmeal on a cold morning, so comforting that we eat it year-round for breakfast or even lunch. And we're telling you that you can make a whack of it, keep it in the refrigerator, nuke it in the morning and have it all week long. Parents, you should eat it too. Oatmeal is full of fibre and iron, it lowers cholesterol, and you can vary it from day to day with different fixings.

You could buy instant oatmeal, but it's expensive, full of sugar and a bit pasty (though definitely better than those sugar cereals). Plus, because the instant variety has been processed and is digested faster than large-flake oatmeal, your kids will be hungry again soon.

8 cups	water
4 cups	large-flake oatmeal (not instant)
¼ tsp	salt
	Milk or cream to taste

Bring water to a boil in a large pot on high heat; add oatmeal and salt. Decrease heat to medium-low; cook, stirring occasionally, for 10 minutes or until water is absorbed and oatmeal is tender. Serve, stirring in milk or cream to suit individual tastes.

Makes 8 servings.

Variations

Oatmeal with Dried Fruit:
Add these to the water as it's heating up. The dates will mostly dissolve to naturally sweeten the oatmeal, and the other dried fruit will plump up. We like how the tang of dried cranberries and apricots offsets the sweetness of the dates, but feel free to use whatever you have on hand. If you have a pair of kitchen scissors, use them to cut up the dried fruit—much easier than using a knife.

$\frac{1}{2}$ cup	chopped dates
$\frac{1}{2}$ cup	dried cranberries
$\frac{1}{2}$ cup	chopped dried apricots
1 tsp	cinnamon

Oatmeal with Fresh Fruit:
Add peeled grated apple or pear to the water as it's heating up, or chopped fresh peaches or other fruit on top when in season.

Extra Power-Protein Oatmeal:
Sprinkle cooked oatmeal with freshly ground flaxseed, toasted wheat germ and chopped nuts.

Oatmeal with Even More Fibre:
Add $\frac{1}{4}$ cup of natural bran during cooking.

Sweet Mystery
"My kids love oatmeal for breakfast, and once they discovered the sweet instant oatmeal packages, there was no looking back. But they eat two packs at a time, and I hate the idea of them eating so much sugar first thing in the morning. So I open a box of regular, unsweetened oatmeal and one of their favourite sugary flavours and mix the packages. They see me putting two in their bowl and are none the wiser."
Suzanne, mother of Owen and Ethan

Granola

Sorry to burst your bubble, but the only reason boxed granola forms delicious big clumps is because it is *loaded* with sugar and fat! This recipe makes truly delicious granola that's really a lot better for you. Feel free to customize the kinds and quantities of nuts and fruit as you wish.

- Unless you are using an industrial-grade juicer, fruit juice does not contain fibre, and, no, the pulp in orange juice is not fibre.
- Apple and grape juices are some of the least nutritious juices available; orange, cranberry and pomegranate are better choices.
- Fruit drinks, beverages and cocktails are not real juice. Look for drinks that are 100 percent juice.
- Check the ingredient list: fruit should be listed first or second, and should definitely come before sugar.
- Up until the age of six, kids should only be having about six ounces of juice daily, so water down their juice as long as you can—maybe until they are teenagers.

3 cups	large-flake oatmeal (not instant)
$\frac{1}{2}$ cup	wheat germ
$\frac{1}{2}$ cup	desiccated unsweetened coconut
$\frac{1}{2}$ cup	chopped pecans or walnuts
$\frac{1}{2}$ cup	hulled unsalted sunflower seeds
$\frac{1}{3}$ cup	vegetable oil
$\frac{1}{4}$ cup	maple syrup
2 tbsp	molasses
$\frac{1}{4}$ tsp	salt
1 cup	dried cranberries or raisins
1 cup	chopped dried apricots

Preheat oven to 350°F.

Combine oatmeal, wheat germ, coconut, pecans or walnuts, and sunflower seeds in a large bowl; toss to combine.

Combine vegetable oil, maple syrup, molasses and salt in a small bowl; pour over oatmeal mixture and mix well to coat.

Pour mixture onto a large rimmed baking sheet; bake for 25 minutes, stirring once, or until granola is lightly toasted. Remove from oven. Stir in cranberries and apricots. Let sit on baking sheet until cool and crisp. Store in an airtight container.

Makes about 7 cups.

Tip: Stored properly, granola should stay fresh for about one month.

Smoothies

Ever notice that kids have an inordinate interest in drinks that come with straws? We take advantage of that with smoothies—it's also a sneaky way of increasing our families' fruit intake without losing the fibre. Fruit is good for parents too, so whip up a blenderful and sip your way to school and work. Needless to say, these also make a great snack.

In the summer, increase the appeal by using frozen fruit, frozen fruit juice or a few ice cubes to chill it down. Little ones may prefer theirs at room temperature.

2 cups	plain or vanilla-flavoured yogurt
3	small bananas, halved
1 ½ cups	fresh or frozen berries or chopped soft fruit (e.g., peaches, kiwi, melon, pear)
½ cup	unsweetened fruit juice (e.g., orange, mango, berry)

Place yogurt, bananas and berries or chopped fruit into a blender; with the motor running on low, add juice a little at a time so there is just enough liquid to help the blades cut through the fruit. The amount of juice needed will depend on the density and juiciness of the fruit used.

Blend until smooth. Pour into 4 glasses to serve.

Makes 4 servings.

Tip: If your children are too little for straws and are drinking their smoothies from sippy cups, you may need to strain out any seeds or bits of fruit skins that did not completely purée, so you don't end up with clogged spouts and frustrated kids.

Tip: Defrost frozen strawberries for a few seconds in the microwave before putting them in the blender, or they end up as hard little lumps.

I'm just not that hungry.

Chapter 5
Lunch: Squeezed at Both Ends

You're coming from one place and heading for another and you realize you have to make something for lunch; or worse, it's 8 a.m. and you are staring at an empty lunch box and an empty fridge.

To help you cope, we suggest you let go of some preconceived ideas. First of all, so-called breakfast and dinner items are perfect for lunch. Oatmeal—great for breakfast *and* lunch. Cold pizza—yum. Chicken fingers with dip—yay!

Kids have pretty good ideas when it comes to bagged lunches, so exploit their opinions on the topic and get them involved. If you work really hard on teaching them how to pack their lunches, you will reach the epitome of freedom: they will do it themselves.

After canvassing lots of kids, we realized that they don't care if they get the same food over and over, as long as they like it to begin with. So if it makes things easier for you, set up a lunch schedule. Mondays are hot dogs, Tuesdays quesadillas, Wednesdays feature soup, etc.—just leave one day for spontaneity (for example, leftovers and the occasional "trying out a new thing").

Nobody wants to fuss too much at lunch—we reserve that for dinner. What you need is something fast and easy. But you can manage to feed your child a variety of foods; it just requires some creative thinking and planning. Soups, interesting sandwiches and quick pastas dominate our lunches, and we have included our favourites here. And the bonus is that they are all things you will enjoy eating too!

Love Your Lunch Box

Mix and match these items for lunch box superiority! Think creatively: cream cheese spread on banana bread, pumpkin seed butter on a tortilla with shredded apple. Sandwich fixings can be packed separately or together—make sure to spread butter or mayo (any fat) on the bread to ward off mushiness. The sky's the limit.

Carbs

- Muffins
- Banana bread
- Apple cinnamon and whole wheat pitas
- Mini bagels
- Bagel chips
- Tortilla chips
- Rice cakes
- Pasta salad
- Rice in a Thermos

Fruits and Veggies

- Sugar snap peas
- Cherry tomatoes
- Green beans
- Cucumber salad
- Shredded veggies
- Coleslaw
- Pickles
- Melon balls with toothpicks
- Watermelon chunks
- Pineapple chunks
- Individual containers of applesauce
- Smoothies in a Thermos
- Dried fruit

Proteins

- Cut-up hot dogs in a Thermos
- Turkey pepperettes
- Exotic deli meats: turkey pastrami, prosciutto, corned beef
- Leftover roast chicken, steak
- Chili in a Thermos
- Hummus, bean dips
- Yogurt in a Thermos (with a bag of granola or berries for sprinkling)
- Cheese strings
- Grated cheese
- Chunks of feta, goat cheese

Sweet Treats

- Cookies
- Brownies
- Caramel rice cakes
- Cheese popcorn
- Fruit bars
- Homemade pudding or Jell-o in a Thermos
- Juice-based gummis
- Natural black licorice

Spreads and Dips

- Cream cheese
- Apple butter
- Jam
- Caesar/ranch dressing
- Hummus
- White bean dip
- Salsa (mix with diced leftover roast chicken or beef and cheese for nachos/burritos)
- Cranberry sauce
- Pumpkin seed butter

Extra, Extra

Next time you're ordering fast food (it's okay, we know we'll bump into you there eventually), pick up extra condiments and dips. They're great to pack in lunch boxes.

Seeking Status

If your child takes lunch to school, then you have a whole other problem to deal with: status. A kid can spot a bad lunch a mile away. Definition of a bad lunch: a sandwich and a piece of fruit. Give your kids a break and pack some currency (by this we mean treats); their social standing may depend on it.

Chicken Stock

Tip: Chicken stock freezes beautifully and can be frozen in small resealable bags so it lies flat in the freezer. Freezing it in ice cube trays and then putting the cubes in a resealable bag is also a handy trick.

Tip: Boil your kids' noodles in stock for a little extra flavour and nutrients.

Tip: Add some egg noodles to your finished broth along with some of the poached meat for the most delicious chicken noodle soup. But be warned—you won't be able to go back to the canned stuff.

We approach chicken stock differently. As is her way, Eshun makes it correctly and gets the most flavour by using a whole chicken. Stock is something you really should get in the habit of making. It is ridiculously easy and makes all your homemade soups and sauces taste better. And the aroma of a stockpot simmering on the stove makes a house a home.

Using a whole chicken leaves you with enough poached chicken to make a pot pie (page 144), a batch of burritos or bowlfuls of chicken salad. But don't be like Emma's bubbe and leave the chicken in so long it becomes inedible.

If you substitute leftover chicken bones (from a roast chicken) or inexpensive parts (backs, necks, wing tips) for a whole chicken, use only as much water as you need to cover them, and simmer for 1 to 2 hours or until stock is full of flavour.

1	3–4 lb chicken
12 cups	cold water
2	onions, unpeeled, quartered
2	carrots, cut into 1-inch pieces
2	leek tops, well rinsed
2	fresh parsley stems (without leaves)

Combine chicken, water, onions, carrots, leek tops and parsley stems in a large pot; bring to a boil. Reduce heat to low and simmer gently for 1 hour.

Remove chicken from pot and set aside until it's cool enough to handle. Remove meat and reserve. Return bones to stock; simmer for 1 hour longer.

Strain stock. Cool. Pour into containers and refrigerate or freeze until needed. Skim fat from surface of chilled stock before using.

Makes about 9 cups stock.

Lunchtime Quickies

- Melts: Everything tastes better with some mild cheese melted on top.
- Smorgasbord: Lay out the odds and ends from the fridge, like cold meats, dips, dressings and pieces of cheese. Use toothpicks for a bonus (if you can trust your kids not to poke their eyes out).
- Toddler heaven: Toddlers love to dip. Child expert Dr. Sears suggests filling an ice cube tray with dips, raw veggies and slices of bread and letting them go crazy.
- Dippy eggs and soldiers: Soft-boiled eggs and toast cut into thin slices to dip into the yolk.
- Purchased vegetable sushi.
- Instant ramen noodles: add veggies and shredded meat.

Alphabet Soup

Even before they can identify the alphabet, kids love to munch on letters, especially the letters of their first name, and inevitably your name too. Maybe it's a Freudian thing. Eshun's son Rory, who says he "hates carrots," is distracted enough by the shape of the noodles to eat them in this soup. That spells W-I-N-N-E-R for us. We cook the noodles right in the broth so they soak up more flavour, but be aware that the starch makes the broth a bit cloudy.

Tip: Alphabet noodles can be found at most health food stores and some supermarkets, but any small shaped noodles will work, including O's, stars, orzo, etc. You will find that the pasta will continue to soak up all the broth as it sits, though, so add a bit of water before attempting to reheat leftovers.

1 tbsp	olive oil
1 cup	chopped onion
1 cup	chopped carrot
1 cup	chopped celery
4 cups	chicken stock
½ cup	alphabet shaped pasta
	Salt and freshly ground pepper

Heat oil in a large pot over medium heat. Add onions, carrots and celery; sauté for 5 minutes or until softened. Add chicken stock and bring to a boil. Add pasta; simmer rapidly for about 8 minutes or until al dente. Season with salt and pepper to taste.

Makes 4 servings.

Martian Soup

For some reason, kids have this idea that they shouldn't like broccoli, but most actually do, and so do we. This pale green soup may appeal because of the funky colour alone, and some vegetable avoiders may even dip their spoon in for a taste. A bonus for the parents: this soup is low in fat.

2 tbsp	unsalted butter
1 ½ cups	chopped onion
5 cups	chicken stock
1 cup	diced peeled Yukon Gold potatoes
4 cups	broccoli florets and peeled, thinly sliced stalks
	Salt and freshly ground pepper

Melt butter in a large pot over medium-low heat. Add onions; sauté for 5 minutes or until lightly golden. Add stock and bring to a boil. Add potatoes; simmer, uncovered, for 10 minutes or until potatoes are tender-crisp. Add broccoli and return to a boil. Reduce heat and simmer for 8 minutes longer or until vegetables are very tender.

Purée soup in a blender for the smoothest texture, or with a hand immersion blender for the quickest cleanup. Return soup to pot and season with salt and pepper to taste.

Makes 4 servings.

Soups *Are* Good Food

There are lots of things that can be puréed, mixed and pulverized into soup without your child ever being the wiser. Soup may be messy, but it's worth it—kids can slurp it out of bowls, mugs or even to-go coffee cups.

Tip: If you're trying to boost your child's iron intake, you could toss in a few handfuls of baby spinach. Let it wilt for 1 minute before puréeing.

Carrot Ginger Soup

Zingy and tangy, carrots and ginger go together like kids and dirt. Maybe it's the hundreds of gingerbread cookies that our boys have ingested—ginger is one of their favourite flavours. There are a lot of nutrients in the carrot peel, so scrub them clean and use them unpeeled if possible.

Tip: This soup is only mildly gingery, in deference to children who don't like things "hot," but it is easy to doctor the adults' soup even after it's cooked. Grate a knob of fresh gingerroot with a rasp or fine grater over a bowl. Squeeze the woody solids to extract fresh ginger "juice," and add enough of this juice to your soup to get the ginger hit you're after.

Tip: Never use powdered ginger in place of fresh gingerroot. Powdered ginger is great for baking. The ugly knobby gingerroot is the one you want for cooking. Buy a knob, throw it in the freezer if you don't think you'll use it up within a week or two, and grate it as you need it.

3 tbsp	unsalted butter
4 cups	sliced unpeeled carrots (2 lb)
1 cup	sliced onion
1 tbsp	chopped gingerroot
6 cups	chicken stock
½ cup	diced peeled potatoes
2 tbsp	whipping cream (optional)
	Salt and freshly ground pepper

Melt butter in a large pot over medium heat. Stir in carrots and onions; cover and cook, stirring occasionally, for 15 minutes or until vegetables are soft and slightly browned. Add gingerroot; sauté for 1 minute more.

Add stock and potatoes; simmer, uncovered, for 15 minutes more or until potatoes are soft. Purée soup in a blender. Stir in cream (if using). Season with salt and pepper to taste.

Makes 4 servings.

Miso Soup

Miso is up there on the health-o-meter. Kids love the slight saltiness of this soup, and if you can convince your kids to eat the tofu, you will get the gold medal for good parenting. We have found that serving this Japanese style is a good incentive: throw out the spoons and slurp it directly from the bowl.

5 cups	water, vegetable stock or chicken stock
1	small carrot, cut into thin strips with a vegetable peeler
1 tbsp	soy sauce
1/4 tsp	sesame oil
1 cup	white miso paste
1/2 cup	cubed silken tofu
4	sheets nori, cut into thin strips

Combine 4 cups water or stock in a large pot along with carrot strips, soy sauce and sesame oil; bring to a boil.

Pour remaining 1 cup hot water or stock into a bowl; stir in miso. Add miso mixture to soup. Add tofu and nori; remove from heat and let stand for 10 minutes or until nori is softened. Stir soup, as it will naturally separate, and serve.

Makes 4 servings.

Shoebox Soup
"Soups are our staple— I could put a shoe in the soup and they would eat it."
Lisa, mother of Zoe and Gabi

Tip: Do not bring the soup to a boil after adding the miso— high heat will kill the healthy bacteria in the fermented soybean paste. Miso paste is available in the refrigerated section of health food stores and some grocery stores.

Tip: The black sheet rolled around sushi is nori. Nori sheets (also called nori paper and nori leaves) are made from seaweed pounded flat. Many large supermarkets and health food stores carry them.

Pasta e Fagioli

An Italian grandmother may not approve of our version of this traditional soup, but we'll put vegetables anywhere we think our kids might enjoy them. The bacon adds great flavour but you can, of course, leave it out if you want to make a vegetarian version. In any case, this is a good, hearty bean and vegetable soup—for lunch or for dinner.

Tip: Whole canned tomatoes have a better consistency and more flavourful juice than pre-chopped canned tomatoes, which is why we prefer them. But chopping canned plum tomatoes is a pain—they ooze juice and make a mess of the cutting board, so Eshun puts the right amount into her liquid measuring cup and squishes up the tomatoes with her hands, or cuts them with scissors. High-quality Italian tomatoes simply fall apart.

4	slices bacon, diced
1 tbsp	olive oil
1 cup	chopped onion
1 cup	chopped carrot
1 cup	chopped celery
½ cup	chopped red pepper
2 tsp	chopped garlic
4 cups	chicken or vegetable stock
1 cup	chopped canned tomatoes with juice
1	19-oz (540 mL) can cannellini or Great Northern beans, drained and well rinsed
½ cup	tubetti or other small pasta
1 tsp	dried oregano
¼ tsp	hot pepper flakes
	Salt and freshly ground pepper
2 tbsp	chopped fresh basil or parsley (optional)
	Grated Parmesan cheese

Heat a large pot over medium heat. Add bacon; sauté for 6 minutes or until crisp. Pour off all but 1 tbsp of the fat. Add olive oil and onions; sauté for 2 minutes or until softened. Add carrots and celery; sauté for 5 minutes or until softened. Add red peppers and garlic; sauté for 1 minute more. Add stock and canned tomatoes; bring to a simmer.

Use a fork to mash half the beans into a rough paste; add to soup along with whole beans, pasta, oregano and hot pepper flakes, stirring to combine.

Simmer soup, uncovered, for 10 minutes or until pasta is al dente and flavours have come together. Season with salt and pepper to taste. Serve sprinkled with basil or parsley, and Parmesan cheese.

Makes 4 servings.

Tip: If you have time to spare, add all the ingredients except the pasta and let simmer for 30 to 45 minutes. Then cook the noodles in the soup for 10 minutes before serving. The flavours will be more mellow and the vegetables softer.

One a Day

We think of lunch as sort of the wedge meal—if we know we are serving something a little bit challenging (i.e., something that the kids are unlikely to eat for dinner), then we try to make lunch very kid-friendly. If one meal is a huge success, it takes the pressure off the others.

Tuna Salad

The first step in making good tuna salad is making good choices at the grocery store. Only buy solid tuna, *never* buy flaked—even at half the price, it's still not worth it. Solid tuna has, gasp, both flavour and texture, and even though you are going to flake it up and add mayo, it matters—a lot.

The salads on these two pages can be made into a delicious sandwich... if your kids eat sandwiches. Ours tend to look at them like they're something that's fallen off the back of a garbage truck—very interesting to dissect, but certainly not to be eaten. That's too bad because we love them (and they're SO easy). If your kids go for sandwiches, don't forget to melt some cheese on top for a delicious treat.

1	6-oz (180 mL) can solid white tuna, packed in water or oil
1/4 cup	mayonnaise
1	green onion, finely chopped
	Salt and freshly ground pepper

Open a can of tuna and use the lid to squeeze out and discard all liquid. (A great treat for your cat.) Scoop tuna into a bowl; add mayonnaise, stirring well to break up all tuna chunks and incorporate mayo. Stir in green onion. Season with salt and pepper to taste.

Makes enough for 2 to 3 sandwiches.

Lunch Date

There is only one lunch that is acceptable when you are catering a play date—plain noodles. You can offer macaroni and cheese, but it probably won't be the same mac and cheese they get at home. Any other choice is doomed to fail. The menu is: plain noodles, carrot sticks, yogurt, fruit, and, if you really want to impress your guests, Popsicles. There is one other option, but use it as a last resort: toast.

Egg Salad

With egg salad, it's all about nicely cooked eggs and good-quality Dijon mustard, which is our subtle way of saying not the bright yellow stuff. And we're willing to share the perfect technique for hard-boiled eggs—no ugly grey ring and not overcooked. Follow it exactly or risk the wrath of Emma's grandmother's spirit.

5	large eggs
¼ cup	mayonnaise
1 tbsp	Dijon mustard
1 tbsp	chopped fresh parsley
	Salt and freshly ground pepper

Place eggs in a small pot with enough water to cover. Bring to a boil, cover pan and remove from heat. Let pan sit for 12 minutes. Drain eggs and rinse with cold water until cool. Peel eggs and grate into a bowl. Add mayonnaise, mustard and parsley; stir gently to combine. Season with salt and pepper to taste.

Makes enough for 2 to 3 sandwiches.

Tip: Egg salad always seems to squish out of your sandwich as you try to eat it. Filling the pocket of a pita bread solves this problem nicely.

Quesadillas

Don't Look Under the Cheese!

Only you know what you can successfully hide in your child's quesadilla, but here are a few suggestions.
- Sliced deli ham or turkey.
- Chopped-up cooked chicken or beef.
- Thinly sliced tomato, zucchini or peppers.
- Grated carrot, a handful of baby spinach.
- Even a smear or small cubes of leftover roasted squash or potato or mashed avocado.

Tip: You can make more quesadillas faster by using large tortillas, but small ones are better for children—since you only need to cut each quesadilla in half (as opposed to in quarters with the large tortillas), the fillings are less likely to fall out.

They're hot, crispy and have melted cheese—what else do you need to know about Mexico's answer to the grilled cheese sandwich? Any leftover meat or veggie can be slipped into the middle of a quesadilla—once it's covered with cheese, anything tastes good. But watch out: if you fill the quesadilla too full, you'll have a hot, gooey mess on your hands.

2	10-inch whole wheat or white (or red, green, speckled with seeds, etc.) flour tortillas, or 4 small tortillas
2 tbsp	salsa, ideally chunky
¼ cup	refried beans (optional) see recipe opposite
¼ cup	grated Cheddar, Monterey Jack or mozzarella cheese
1 tbsp	vegetable oil
	Salsa and sour cream

Lay tortillas on the counter and spread half of each with salsa and refried beans (if using). Sprinkle cheese evenly over salsa and bean mixture; fold tortillas in half to cover fillings. Press down to "seal."

Heat a frying or grill pan over medium-high heat; brush surface with vegetable oil.

Add quesadillas to pan; fry or grill for about 2 minutes per side or until cheese is melted and quesadillas are crisp.

Cut into wedges and serve with salsa and sour cream or, in a pinch, ketchup and plain yogurt.

Makes 2 to 4 quesadillas.

Refried Beans

Okay, this makes a lot, but it lasts at least a week and is a great thing to have in your fridge. Serve it with eggs for breakfast, in burritos or quesadillas, or on nachos. Or thin it out with water, yogurt or sour cream and turn it into a dip. Kids, even babies, love it any which way, and it's packed with protein and fibre.

2 tbsp	olive oil
1 cup	chopped onion
1 tbsp	chopped garlic
1 tsp	ground cumin
1 tsp	ground coriander
1/4 tsp	chili flakes
2	19-oz (540 mL) cans Mexican red, pinto, kidney or black beans, well rinsed and drained
3/4 cup	water
	Salt and freshly ground pepper

Heat oil in a frying pan over medium heat. Add onions; sauté for 5 minutes or until browned. Turn heat to medium-low; add garlic and cook, stirring, for 1 minute or until pale golden. Stir in cumin, coriander and chili flakes; cook for 30 seconds or until fragrant.

Add beans and water to the pan; simmer for 8 minutes or until beans are very soft. Remove from heat. Using a potato masher, mash beans to whatever texture you desire. If you like it drier, cook it slightly longer; if soupier, add a little water. Season with salt and pepper to taste.

Makes 3 cups.

Grate Idea

Graham buys a big block of cheese and then grates half of it with the box grater. The grated cheese goes in a resealable bag (which can be kept in the freezer) and is ready for Julia and Paige's pizzas and pastas, and for sprinkling on vegetables. The big whack of cheese might be a bit pricey, but we're willing to bet that if you did the math, you'd find it's still cheaper than buying the pre-shredded stuff, and there's just no denying that it tastes far superior.

Tip: If you are buying a can of refried beans, read the ingredients carefully to make sure it does not contain any trans fats. Don't even think about using the packaged dry mixes unless you're going camping—texturally they don't come close to the real thing.

I'm Allergic to Green

Chapter 6
Snacks: Time Out!

Kids need to snack—their bodies are growing at the speed of light, and they need to recharge those batteries every few hours. If you have a picky eater, main meals can seem like a total write-off, so snacks become *very* important. Try to think of snack time as a perfect opportunity to give your kids some healthy nutrients without them even noticing.

In theory, kids should be having structured mid-morning, mid-afternoon and possibly, depending on how early they eat dinner, a bedtime snack each day. And these snacks would not be in any kind of moving vehicle or in front of any electronic babysitting appliance. Back in the real world, our kids snack in some of the craziest places (top of the slide, anyone?).

Snack time is not the time to completely abandon any attempts at healthy eating, but it's also not a time to harp on the building blocks of good nutrition. So how do you strike a balance? Keep snack time fun and casual, give your kids things they like, chuck in some healthy stuff and don't make a big deal out of it.

We've included some of our favourite snacks here, and as a bonus, most of the baked goods in this chapter can also be considered dessert, or even breakfast on the go.

Our Favourite Dried Apricot Bars

In Emma's house, these are called "My Favourite Thing" because they are Zachary's snack and dessert of choice—of course, he likes chocolate chips and dried cranberries in his. In Eshun's house, this is her husband's breakfast on the go, minus the chocolate chips. We don't tell either of them that they are quite a healthy snack.

If you're in a hurry or your apricots are very soft and fresh, you can skip the step of simmering them in sweetened water, but it does make the bars moister.

1 cup	chopped dried apricots
¾ cup	water
2 tbsp	sugar
1 cup	packed dark brown sugar
2	large eggs
½ cup	vegetable oil
1 tsp	vanilla
1 ½ cups	large-flake oatmeal (not instant)
1 cup	all-purpose flour
½ cup	wheat germ
½ tsp	baking powder
½ tsp	cinnamon
½ tsp	salt
½ cup	dried cranberries and/or chocolate chips (optional)

Party in a Bag

Kids fighting? Harassing you when you want to make phone calls? Grumpy? Take all the things your kids like—pretzels, Cheerios and other cereals, raisins, dried cranberries, even those fish crackers. Add some things they aren't sure of, like pumpkin seeds, sunflower seeds and almonds, and throw in a teensy-weensy amount of chocolate chips. Then hope they will eat the healthy sweet-and-salty mix while searching for the chocolate chips.

Place apricots, water and sugar in a small saucepan; bring to a boil. Reduce heat to medium and simmer for 20 minutes or until apricots are tender and most of the water has been absorbed. Drain and reserve apricots.

Preheat oven to 350°F.

Line the base of an 8-inch square baking pan with parchment paper.

Combine brown sugar, eggs, vegetable oil and vanilla in a large bowl. Mix in oatmeal. Set aside.

Combine flour, wheat germ, baking powder, cinnamon and salt in a small bowl; stir with a fork to blend. Add to oatmeal mixture, stirring to combine. Stir in reserved apricots and dried cranberries or chocolate chips, if using.

Spread mixture in prepared pan. Bake for 35 minutes or until lightly browned. Cool completely before cutting into squares.

Makes 16 2-inch bars.

A Message from Your Dentist

Your dentist, your doctor and your kids may have differing opinions on some snack foods. If it were up to the dentist, your kids would never eat dried fruit, crackers or gummis, never drink juice in the middle of the day or in bed, never suck on lollipops and never, ever touch fruit leather. Your doctor (if he or she is at all like ours) may be a serious advocate of iron-filled dried apricots. Hard cheese is one thing everyone would agree on. It's a fabulous snack and contains good bacteria that eat away at all those gross "sugar bugs."

Banana Chocolate Oatmeal Bread

Dr. Freeze and the Banana

Isn't it amazing how quickly bananas can go from beautiful bright yellow creations to stinky brown tubes of mush? At which point you promise yourself you will make banana bread, but after a few days of looking at them guiltily, you toss them in the freezer, peel and all. And then you have bags of dark brown lumps taking up space. Try this instead: When the aroma of overripe banana fills the kitchen, peel them, put them in a freezer storage bag and mash them flat. Now they will lie flat in your freezer. Keep adding to the bag until the day you actually do make banana bread or smoothies. Defrost what you need by placing the bag in warm water. Drain off the excess liquid before using. A half cup of frozen mashed banana is equal to about one medium banana.

Baking is often a last-minute "What am I going to do with the kids on this rainy day?" or "I'd like to avoid doing laundry" kind of thing, which means we don't usually plan well enough to have taken the butter out of the fridge or freezer in time to get it to room temperature. So any recipe that calls for melted butter means you don't have to walk around with two sticks of butter softening in your back pocket. This is the banana bread recipe you have been looking for: soft, moist, loaded with bananas, a bit of oatmeal for good health and chocolate for added kid appeal.

¾ cup	sugar
½ cup	unsalted butter, melted
2	large eggs
½ cup	quick-cooking oatmeal
1 ½ cups	mashed banana (3–4 very ripe bananas)
¼ cup	buttermilk
1 tsp	vanilla
1 ½ cups	all-purpose flour
1 tsp	baking soda
½ tsp	salt
⅓ cup	chocolate chips

Preheat oven to 350°F.

Grease and flour a loaf pan.

Combine sugar and butter in a large bowl and stir until uniform. Add eggs, one at a time, and stir to incorporate. Add oats, banana, buttermilk and vanilla; stir until uniform.

Combine flour, baking soda and salt in a small bowl; stir with a fork to blend.

Add flour mixture to banana mixture one third at a time; stir until just combined. Stir in chocolate chips.

Pour batter into prepared pan. Bake for 1 hour to 1 hour and 10 minutes or until loaf is dark brown and a cake tester comes out clean. Cool bread in pan for 10 minutes, then run a knife along the edges to loosen, turn out of baking pan and cool on a rack.

Makes 1 loaf.

Tip: Yes, you can also make this into muffins—bake muffins for 20 minutes. You'll get about 12 muffins or 20 mini muffins.

Tip: If you are only going to purchase one kind of oatmeal, you should buy the old-fashioned, or large-flake oatmeal. To turn them into the "quick-cooking" oatmeal we call for in this recipe, pulse them in a food processor, or place in a resealable plastic bag and rub them between your hands until they're broken into small bits.

Blueberry Cornmeal Muffins

Buttermilk Basics

Buttermilk figures prominently in our recipes because it makes everything lighter. But people are often afraid to buy it because they think it will just sit and go sour in the fridge. But buttermilk is already sour and it lasts about a month after its best-before date. It's supposed to smell slightly off and be a bit chunky, so shake before using. And though it sounds fatty, buttermilk is only 1% fat. But if we can't convince you, then substitute thinned plain yogurt or add a tablespoon of vinegar to one cup of milk and let it sit for five minutes. Buttermilk powder is also available. The results won't be quite as light and fluffy, but only you will know the difference.

Blueberry muffins are the world's favourite muffin, or at least our kids' favourite. These ones have a little cornmeal, which solves that icky, doughy taste that store-bought muffins often have. And it also uses up some of that big bag of cornmeal you bought for the bottom of the pizza stone, which you never use (not to mention the homemade polenta that you were going to whip up a few months back).

2 cups	all-purpose flour
1 cup	cornmeal
¾ cup	sugar
1 tbsp	baking powder
1 tsp	baking soda
½ tsp	salt
1 ½ cups	fresh or frozen blueberries
1 ½ cups	buttermilk
3	large eggs, beaten
¾ cup	vegetable oil
½ tsp	vanilla
½ tsp	grated lemon rind

Preheat oven to 350°F.

Grease a muffin pan or line with muffin papers.

Combine flour, cornmeal, sugar, baking powder, baking soda and salt in a medium bowl; stir with a fork to blend. Add blueberries and toss to coat with flour mixture.

Combine buttermilk, eggs, vegetable oil, vanilla and lemon rind in a separate bowl. Add flour mixture to buttermilk mixture and stir until just combined.

Spoon batter into a muffin pan (filling the cups ¾ full). Bake for 20 minutes or until muffins are lightly golden at edges and baked through.

Makes 18 muffins or 30 mini muffins.

Tip: If you are going to go through the process of making muffins, we believe it's worth making a lot and freezing some. They can easily be rewarmed from frozen in a 350°F oven or toaster oven for instant "freshness."

Silpat Saved My Life

There is a totally amazing invention out there that will change your life, or at least make baking a lot easier, and isn't that the same thing? The original brand name is Silpat by Demarle—bakeware made of silicone and fibreglass that is totally nonstick and can be heated to searing temperatures. Using fibreglass baking sheets means no more greasing cookie sheets, no more crumbled, stuck cookies, and you can even roll out dough on them. Unbelievable muffin tins are also available. Say goodbye to muffin papers littering your floor. The muffins pop right out, and cleanup is a breeze. A word of warning: place the muffin tin on a light-coloured cookie sheet before putting it in the oven or it will be very hard to take out. We'll be honest; they're expensive. There are cheaper knock-offs, but we have not had as much luck with them. And aren't you worth it?

Really Yummy and Not Just Healthy Carrot Bran Muffins

Eshun's Baking Tips

Cooking is intuitive but baking is a science. To properly measure dry ingredients, always use the appropriate measuring utensil and never, never scoop out the ingredient with the measuring cup (we know you've done it). Instead, spoon the dry ingredient into the graduated measuring cup, levelling it off with your finger or a knife, and do not pack it down. Also, always use a liquid measuring cup for wet ingredients. If the ingredients aren't measured properly, everything will just be a little bit off, which could mean the difference between success and failure.

While testing bran muffin recipes, Eshun had a flash of realization: she doesn't like bran muffins. But the rational side of her brain said we had to have a healthy bran muffin recipe. And then Eshun made these ones and she liked them, and so did the kids. You will probably like them too, just not as much as that coffee shop cupcake masquerading as a muffin.

1 cup	natural bran
1 cup	buttermilk
2	large eggs, beaten
½ cup	unsweetened applesauce
⅓ cup	vegetable oil
¾ cup	lightly packed dark brown sugar
1 ¼ cups	all-purpose flour
½ cup	whole wheat flour
2 tsp	baking powder
1 ½ tsp	baking soda
1 tsp	cinnamon
½ tsp	salt
1 ½ cups	finely grated carrot
½ cup	chopped pitted dates, raisins or dried cranberries

Preheat oven to 400°F.

Grease a muffin pan or line with muffin papers.

Place bran in a large bowl. Pour buttermilk, eggs, applesauce and oil over bran; stir to combine. Add brown sugar and stir until uniform.

Combine flours, baking powder, baking soda, cinnamon and salt in a small bowl; stir with a fork to blend. Stir in grated carrot and dates; mix until coated with flour mixture. Add flour mixture to bran mixture; stir until just combined.

Spoon batter into muffin pan (filling the cups ¾ full). Bake for 20 to 22 minutes or until a tester comes out clean.

Makes 18 muffins or 30 mini muffins.

Tip: If you think you can get away with having green flecks in your muffins, you can substitute 1 cup of grated zucchini for the carrots. Adding 2 tsp of ground ginger is a nice accompaniment.

Muffin Mix Made Marvellous

Store-bought muffin mix is made as idiot-proof as possible, which means you can add all sorts of crazy things to it. We tend to like the mixes that list only ingredients we can pronounce.

Some things you can do to up the nutritional content and flavour of your muffin mix:

- Add 1 cup grated carrots or zucchini, mashed banana or berries, or canned pumpkin.
- Substitute applesauce for the oil.
- Add dried or fresh cranberries and even a little lemon zest.
- Chuck in some chocolate chips.
- Replace half of the water with buttermilk (makes them lighter in texture).
- Add 1/4 cup wheat germ for a health boost.

Roasted Chickpeas

Snack Day Panic Attack

Nothing elicits panic like the pressure of having to bring the snack for your child's class. For us, it usually coincides with the day after we've been up all night with a crying baby. Eshun coordinates snack-time at Rory's preschool, where they stress the importance of serving snacks that contain protein, carbs and fruit or veg. Cheese, whole grain crackers and sliced apples are the big winners, but they've managed to come up with inventive substitutions like cream cheese on raisin pitas, yogurt, devilled eggs, cheese tortellini, apricot squares, mini muffins, sugar snap peas and canned baby corn.

Okay, it's not potato chips, but anything this easy and healthy is worth trying out on your kids. Just think of how much protein and fibre you'll be able to get into them if they like these crunchy little balls. And if they do like them, double the recipe the next time round.

1	19-oz (540 mL) can chickpeas, drained and rinsed
1 tbsp	olive oil
½ tsp	ground cumin
½ tsp	brown sugar
½ tsp	salt

Preheat oven to 375°F.

Combine chickpeas, olive oil, cumin, brown sugar and salt in a medium bowl; toss to coat.

Spread chickpeas on a baking sheet. Bake for 35 to 40 minutes or until chickpeas are dry to the touch and slightly golden.

Makes 2 cups.

Tip: Use caution serving these to children under three as they may be a choking hazard.

Hermit Cookies

These are dark and gingerbread-y—a soft, cakey cookie full of dried fruit and iron-rich molasses. Eshun has a thing against raisins (but loves dates, hence the number of recipes with dates in them). Many kids might agree, feeling that any option is better than raisins (sometimes referred to as flies or slugs), including currants, dried apricots and chopped dates.

½ cup	currants or raisins
½ cup	dried cranberries
1 cup	boiling water
½ cup	unsalted butter, softened
1 cup	sugar
½ cup	molasses
2	eggs
2 cups	all-purpose flour
¾ cup	whole wheat flour
1 tsp	baking soda
1 ½ tsp	ground ginger
1 tsp	cinnamon
½ tsp	ground nutmeg
½ tsp	ground cloves
½ tsp	salt

Preheat oven to 350°F.

Line 2 baking sheets with parchment paper.

Soak currants and dried cranberries in boiling water for 10 minutes or until plump and soft. Drain and place on a paper towel to dry. Reserve.

Combine butter and sugar in a medium bowl; beat until light and fluffy. Add molasses and beat until incorporated. Beat in eggs, one at a time.

Combine flours, baking soda, ginger, cinnamon, nutmeg, cloves and salt in a separate bowl; stir with a fork to blend.

Add flour mixture to butter mixture and stir until just combined. Mix in reserved dried fruit.

Drop by tablespoonfuls (2 tbsp per cookie), about 2 inches apart, onto prepared baking sheets. Bake cookies, one baking sheet at a time, for 18 minutes or until cookies are just firm to the touch. Allow cookies to cool for 5 minutes before transferring them to a rack to cool completely.

Makes 18 large cookies.

Just a Wee Bit Healthier Chocolate Chip Cookies

Making truly healthy cookies would be a waste of time—who would eat them? So we've adulterated the childhood favourite just enough to justify serving it for a snack. We love these cookies—you be the judge.

1 cup	unsalted butter, softened
3/4 cup	sugar
1 cup	packed light brown sugar
3	large eggs
2 tsp	vanilla
2 1/2 cups	all-purpose flour
1 cup	large-flake oatmeal (not instant)
1/2 cup	wheat germ
1 tsp	baking soda
1 tsp	salt
2 cups	chocolate chips
1 cup	dried cranberries

Preheat oven to 350°F.

Line 2 baking sheets with parchment paper.

Combine butter and sugars in a large bowl; beat with an electric mixer until light and fluffy.

Add eggs, one at a time, beating well between additions. Add vanilla and beat to incorporate.

Combine flour, oatmeal, wheat germ, baking soda and salt in a medium bowl; stir with a fork to combine. Add flour mixture to butter mixture and beat until just combined. Stir in chocolate chips and cranberries.

Drop walnut-sized balls of dough onto prepared baking sheets, about 2 inches apart, and flatten slightly. Bake cookies, one baking sheet at a time, for 15 minutes or until cookies are pale golden and just firm to the touch. Allow cookies to cool for 5 minutes or until firm, then transfer to a rack to cool completely.

Makes 36 cookies.

Almond Tea Cake

Sometimes you just have a hankering for a bit of cake—nothing glamorous with icing, just something plain and tasty. And this is it. Of course, kids will eat anything that has the word cake in it. Just don't tell your nut-phobic child what it is until they've tried it and fallen in love. It's a moist cake, so if you don't eat the whole thing at one sitting, wrap it in plastic and it will keep for a few days.

This cake tastes most sublime when you toast the almonds and grind them yourself, but substitute 1 1/4 cups ground almonds if you prefer.

5 oz/1 cup	whole natural almonds
1 cup	sugar
1/2 cup	all-purpose flour
1/2 tsp	baking powder
1/4 tsp	salt
1/2 cup	unsalted butter, softened
3	large eggs
2 tsp	grated lemon rind
1/4 tsp	almond extract

Preheat oven to 350°F.

Butter and flour the sides of an 8-inch round cake pan and line the bottom with a piece of parchment paper.

Place almonds on a baking sheet and roast for 8 minutes or until they smell toasty. Cool. Place almonds in a food processor along with 1/3 cup of the sugar; pulse until finely ground. Reserve.

Combine flour, baking powder and salt in a small bowl; stir with a fork to blend.

Combine butter and remaining 2/3 cup sugar (or entire 1 cup sugar if using pre-ground almonds) in a large bowl; beat with an electric mixture until light and fluffy. Add eggs, one at a time, beating well between additions. Add lemon rind and almond extract; beat until combined. Add reserved ground almonds; beat until uniform. Add flour mixture to butter mixture; beat until just incorporated.

Spread batter in prepared pan. Bake for 35 minutes or until top is golden. Cool in pan for 10 minutes. Use a knife to loosen cake from sides of pan, then transfer to a rack to cool completely.

Makes 6 servings.

Oatmeal Scones

The "Trick or Treat?" Awards

Stephen's kids are convinced that Orangina is a forbidden treat reserved for restaurants and illnesses only. They treasure it more than pop.

Sasha thinks raisins are candy, and Bethany was convinced that the Easter bunny only brought plastic eggs filled with raisins, apricots and dried prunes.

Judy convinced Maddy that a banana split is a banana with the contents of a mini yogurt plopped on top and a tiny amount of sprinkles. In fact, Judy advocates the generous use of sprinkles as an enticement on many dishes.

And the winner is Sally. Her son thinks V8 is a treat, yes, V8. Way to go, Sally!

Okay, we're going to come clean here: the oatmeal in these scones ensures that they are not the lightest, creamiest biscuits you have ever had (for those, see Shortcakes on page 167), but it does make them healthier than most. You can make them bleary-eyed on a Saturday morning because eating something straight from the oven will always make you feel good, no matter how bad you actually feel. These scones are also extremely versatile—they can be made into cranberry scones, cheese biscuits and even chicken pot pie topping. Make them right now.

1 cup	large-flake oatmeal (not instant)
¾ cup	buttermilk
1 ½ cups	all-purpose flour
1 tsp	baking powder
¼ tsp	baking soda
½ tsp	salt
½ cup	cold unsalted butter, cut into pieces
¼ cup	packed light brown sugar

Topping:

1	egg
2 tbsp	milk
1 tsp	sugar (optional)

Preheat oven to 375°F.

Line a baking sheet with parchment paper.

Combine oatmeal and buttermilk in a small bowl. Stir to moisten oatmeal and let soak while you assemble the rest of the ingredients.

Combine flour, baking powder, baking soda and salt in a large bowl; stir with a fork to blend. Add butter and brown sugar. Using your fingers or a pastry blender, work mixture until butter is the size of small peas.

Mix oatmeal mixture into flour mixture, stirring to break up clumps of oatmeal until just combined and dough becomes slightly sticky and shaggy looking.

Turn out dough onto a lightly floured surface and pat into a round about 1 inch thick. Cut dough into 6 to 8 wedges and place on baking sheet.

Topping: Beat egg with milk and brush over tops and sides of scones. Sprinkle tops with sugar if desired.

Bake for 25 minutes or until scones are golden brown and cooked through.

Makes 6 to 8 scones.

Tip: To make cheese biscuits, follow the recipe, cutting the sugar down to one tablespoon and adding 1/2 cup grated cheese.

To make a topping for Chicken Pot Pie (pages 144–45), roll out the dough thinly on a lightly floured surface.

Sauce makes my knees hurt

Chapter 7
The Picky Eater Hall of Fame

In the same way adults commit to a food strategy—low-carb diet, anyone?—kids can get attached to a food notion and never budge from it. Sometimes it's the fat-and-sugar diet; often it's the popular white-food diet.

Around three, even the most adventurous eater may go through a phase where only one type of food will do. When the kids have dug in their heels and refuse to try anything new, we call this phase "scraping the bottom of the barrel." You know what we mean. It means you're opening up the freezer and pulling out chicken fingers, or boiling up noodles each and every day.

One way to feel better about what your kids are eating is to know exactly what goes into their food (and being able to spell all the ingredients). To that end, we are offering up our own recipes for some kid classics. Some are just as easy as the frozen or packaged version. All of them taste a lot better than their ready-made counterparts and will introduce your children to true flavours, instead of synthetic ones. You have to start somewhere. These recipes will ensure everyone is eating tasty and delicious flavours and textures while you gradually work on opening up your kids' eyes to the amazing world of food.

Beyond Boxed Macaroni and Cheese

Supertasters

Able to taste teeny shreds of onion hidden in spaghetti sauce, able to sniff out supplements in juice, able to find bitter tastes in any dish—it's Supertaster! Scientists have discovered that about 25 percent of the population are supertasters. Supertasters have more taste buds on their tongue and tastes are stronger to them, especially bitterness. Children are born supertasters. This may have been an evolutionary defence against poisonous foods. While we would obviously call ourselves super-tasters based on our uncanny ability to taste the slightest hint of margarine in any dish, we believe our kids use their supertasting skills for evil instead of good.

Mac and cheese does not need a long intro. It is what it is. We have served this dish at parties as kids' food, but the adults ate it all.

Don't forget that orange and white cheeses make differently coloured sauces. And while we adults love old sharp Cheddar, the children don't always agree, so go with the house favourite. And don't underestimate the appeal of this dish cooked in small ramekins—kids love to have their own special portion.

1 lb	macaroni, penne or other short tubular pasta
¼ cup	unsalted butter
1 cup	chopped onion
1 tbsp	chopped garlic
⅓ cup	all-purpose flour
4 cups	hot milk
1 tbsp	Dijon mustard
3 ½ cups	grated Cheddar cheese
	Salt and freshly ground pepper
2 cups	fresh bread crumbs
¼ cup	freshly grated Parmesan cheese
2 tbsp	olive oil

Preheat oven to 350°F.

Bring a large pot of salted water to a boil; add pasta and cook according to package directions until al dente. Drain.

Heat butter in a large saucepan over medium heat while pasta is cooking. Add onion and garlic; sauté for 2 minutes or until softened. Add flour and combine with butter to make a smooth paste. Cook, stirring constantly, for 2 minutes. Slowly whisk in hot milk. Continue whisking until milk has come to a boil and thickened. Remove pot from heat. Whisk in mustard. Add cheese, a handful at a time, and mix well. Season with salt and pepper to taste.

Combine pasta and sauce; spoon into an oiled 9- x 13-inch baking dish or a variety of individual oiled baking dishes.

Combine bread crumbs with Parmesan in a medium bowl. Add olive oil and toss to moisten crumbs. Season with salt and pepper. Sprinkle crumbs evenly over pasta.

Bake for 35 minutes or until sauce is bubbling and crumbs are golden.

Makes 4 to 6 servings.

Tip: This is also great with a can or two of tuna mixed in, or a few cups of baby spinach, cooked broccoli or peas.

Tip: Don't be embarrassed by your love for boxed mac and cheese. It can't be beat for ease and kid appeal. Our fabulous photographer, Jenna, showed us how to beef up the nutritional content by adding an egg to the sauce before adding it to the noodles. She whisks in an egg with the milk and stirs continuously over low heat until hot, then she adds the cheese powder and butter.

A Better Red Pasta Sauce

We've snuck a few extra vitamin-packed vegetables into this sauce that your child won't be able to discern and that, happily, add to the orangey-red colour and sweet homogeneous (but we don't mean bland!) flavour kids love. It takes a while to cook but doesn't need to be watched, so get on with life as it simmers.

2 tbsp	olive oil
1 cup	chopped onion
½ cup	chopped carrot
1 cup	diced red pepper
1 tsp	chopped garlic
1	28-oz (828 mL) can Italian plum tomatoes
½–1 cup	water (optional)
	Salt and freshly ground pepper
1 tbsp	unsalted butter

Heat olive oil in a large saucepan over medium heat.

Add onions and carrots; sauté for 5 minutes or until onions are translucent. Add peppers and garlic; sauté for 2 minutes more or until peppers are softened.

Add canned tomatoes to the pan with their juices; use a wooden spoon to break them up slightly. Cover, turn down heat to low and simmer for 50 minutes or until carrots are very tender.

Purée mixture in a blender or food processor along with enough water to achieve desired consistency. Return sauce to pan and season with salt and pepper to taste. Stir butter into sauce just before serving to sweeten and mellow the flavour.

Makes 3 to 4 cups, or enough to coat about 1 ½ lb dry pasta.

Tip: Make a double or even triple recipe and freeze it for future family dinners. Try freezing it in small resealable bags, laid flat, for instant kid meals.

Tip: All children have preferences when it comes to pasta shapes. To make the most of the pasta sauce as a vegetable serving, use a shape that "holds" the sauce well, like radiatore, rigatoni or orecchiette.

Ultimate White Pasta

Did you know there was a proper way to do plain pasta with cheese? The trick is to add the cheese and butter a bit at a time while tossing the pasta so that the cheese dissolves as the butter melts and becomes just enough of a "sauce" to cling to the pasta. We promise you that the entire family will enjoy this, but try not to make it a daily occurrence. You may want to serve some garlicky sautéed greens or a bowl of chopped fresh tomatoes, or diced chicken or ham, and herbs on the side for the adults or more adventurous children to mix in.

1 lb	spaghetti or other long pasta
1 ¼ cup	freshly grated Parmesan cheese
¼ cup	unsalted butter, cut into cubes
	Freshly ground pepper

Bring a large pot of salted water to a boil. Add spaghetti and cook according to package directions until al dente. Drain, reserving ½ cup pasta cooking water.

Return pasta to the still-warm pot; add ⅓ of the cheese and toss pasta rapidly to distribute. Add half of the butter, another ⅓ of the cheese and continue tossing. Add remaining butter, cheese and enough reserved pasta cooking water to loosen; toss until well combined. Serve immediately, and pass the pepper to the grown-ups.

Makes 4 servings.

Butter Diatribe

When we call for butter we always mean unsalted butter. Salted butter contains more water, which generally messes up baking directions and alters the seasonings of a recipe. The only time salted butter is good is when it is slathered on toast. And if you think we dislike salted butter, don't even get us started on the topic of margarine.

Real Cheese, Please

Your kids deserve the best so why are you sprinkling those flakey bits of cardboard on their pasta? Parmigiano-Reggiano is the Queen of Italian Cheese and deserves better treatment. Try a wedge of authentic Parmesan and grate it at home—you will be introducing your kids to real cheese flavour.

Chicken Fingers

Panko Very Much

Panko, also called Japanese bread crumbs, is the best crunchy coating out there, because the crumbs have already been fried. They are coarser in texture than regular bread crumbs and can be purchased at Asian grocery stores and some supermarkets. Many brands have trans fat in them, but organic, trans fat–free panko is becoming more and more available at health food stores.

Tip: Instead of frying them in oil, you can bake the chicken fingers in a 425°F oven. Place chicken fingers on an oiled baking sheet and bake for 10 minutes, turning after 5 minutes, or until coating is browned and crisp and chicken is cooked through.

It would be impossible to calculate just how many chicken fingers Max ate in the first four years of his life. Despite Eshun's best efforts to tempt him with other forms of protein, they continued to be a staple of his diet, so she became very adept at making batches of them at home. The secret: they need to be well seasoned and crispy.

Use chicken free of hormones and antibiotics whenever possible, whole wheat bread for the bread crumbs for extra fibre and olive oil for the cooking, and you'll feel a bit less guilty about what your child is eating for dinner. Use the exact same method to make fish sticks (use sole, halibut, cod), and if you tell them it's chicken, well, that's up to you.

1 lb	boneless, skinless chicken breasts (about 2 large)
½ cup	all-purpose flour
½ tsp	chili powder
	Salt and freshly ground pepper
1	large egg
2 tbsp	milk
3 cups	fresh bread crumbs (from about 5 slices of bread) or panko
¼ cup	olive oil for frying

Cut chicken breasts against the grain to make slices just under ½-inch thick.

Combine flour, chili powder, and salt and pepper on a large plate.

Mix egg and milk in a shallow bowl with a pinch of salt; beat until mixture is uniform.

Place bread crumbs on a large plate; season with salt and pepper to taste.

Working in batches, toss chicken in flour mixture; dip into egg mixture to moisten; then toss in crumbs, pressing down slightly to fully coat. Freeze any chicken fingers you want to save for another day on a parchment-lined cookie sheet; once frozen, transfer to airtight, resealable bags.

Heat 2 tbsp of the olive oil in a frying pan over medium heat. Add chicken fingers; fry for about 1 ½ minutes per side or until coating is browned and crisp and chicken is cooked through, adding more oil to pan as needed. (If you are cooking frozen chicken fingers, use low heat and cook for about 4 minutes per side.)

Makes about 20 chicken fingers.

Honey Mustard Dipping Sauce

Mix together 1/2 cup honey and 2 tbsp Dijon mustard for a simple and healthy alternative to that nasty plum sauce.

Stale Solutions

Have the odd leftover hamburger bun, stale English muffin or ends of a loaf of bread? You've got the makings of your own bread crumbs. Throw them in a bag in your freezer until you've gathered a bunch, thaw slightly and then run them through the food processor. Pop the crumbs into a resealable bag, put them back into the freezer until you need them, and you will feel impressively frugal!

Whole Wheat Pizza Dough

You may have heard it before, but pizza truly is the perfect food. You've got all your food groups combined in one delicious kid-friendly package, and you'd be amazed at the amount of vegetables you can hide under the cheese.

Even those kids who don't eat pizza will enjoy the project of making pizza dough, and it also gives them freedom to decide on their own toppings. Zachary makes breadsticks and dips them into olive oil. Max has a "white" pizza with no sauce, just olive oil, garlic, carrots and broccoli (we don't know where he came up with that combo).

Sautéing the onions and vegetables before adding them to the pizza really softens them up, but you can get away with slicing everything very thinly. You can play with the proportions of whole wheat and white flour.

$\frac{1}{4}$ cup	warm water
1 tbsp	active dry yeast
2 cups	all-purpose flour
1 cup	whole wheat flour
$\frac{2}{3}$ cup	cold water
$\frac{1}{4}$ cup	olive oil
1 tsp	salt

Quick Pizzas

If you have tomato sauce and cheese in the fridge, almost anything can be turned into a super-fast pizza. Bagel pizzas, English muffin pizzas, baguette pizzas, pita pizzas and even crackers can turn into mini-mini-pizzas.

Suggested Toppings

- Cheese and more cheese— mozzarella, Cheddar, feta, goat cheese
- Pepperoni, bacon, leftover chicken
- Thin slices of potato
- Spinach
- Pineapple
- Broccoli
- Pesto
- Mushrooms
- Roasted red peppers
- Zucchini

(see over)

Tip: A lesson learned from a popular takeout pizza place: roll the dough right onto a piece of parchment paper, where it will stick like glue, allowing you to make it really thin. Prick the dough with a fork to keep it from forming bubbles. Assemble your pizza. Using the back of a baking sheet, slide it onto a pizza stone in the oven, parchment and all. The dough cooks before the paper has a chance to burn, and the pizza separates from the paper as it cooks. Watch any extra overhanging paper though—this can scorch.

Tip: Pizza dough freezes beautifully—just seal portions in resealable bags and defrost at room temperature before using.

Place warm water in the bowl of your mixer and sprinkle yeast into water. Let stand for 5 minutes or until yeast has mostly dissolved.

Add all-purpose and whole wheat flours, water, olive oil and salt to yeast mixture; combine on low speed using a dough hook until dough has formed a ball. (Depending on the humidity of the air, you may need to add 1 to 2 tbsp more flour or water to create a soft, elastic dough that is not sticky.)

Place dough in a clean, oiled bowl; cover with plastic wrap and place in a warm spot for 45 minutes or until it has risen to double its size. Punch dough down and divide in half, or in quarters for individual pizzas.

Roll out each ball of dough as thinly as possible on a lightly floured surface; slide onto a cookie sheet, prick with a fork and add toppings.

Preheat oven to 500°F, and if you have a pizza stone, put it on the lowest rack of your oven.

Turn down oven to 450°F when you are ready to bake. Cook pizzas, one at a time, on lowest rack for 20 minutes or until crust is browned on bottom and cheese is bubbling.

Makes 4 servings.

Fried Rice

Emma's amazing nanny, Jannet, has been feeding Noah fried rice since he began eating solids. Protein from the egg, along with the veggies and rice, makes this a perfect one-pot dish, ensuring Noah got used to eating food that was all mixed together. He has avoided the all-white diet ever since.

1 tbsp	vegetable oil
2 tsp	chopped garlic
4 cups	cold cooked rice
¾ cup	frozen peas
½ cup	grated carrots
2	large eggs, beaten with pinch of salt
1 cup	diced or shredded cooked chicken, ham or tofu
2 tbsp	soy sauce
	Freshly ground pepper

Heat oil in a large frying pan over medium heat. Add garlic; sauté for 1 minute. Add rice, peas and carrots; stir-fry for 2 to 3 minutes, breaking up rice with a spoon.

Using the spoon, make a well in the rice, exposing the bottom of the pan. Add eggs and mix through the rice; cook, stirring, for 1 to 2 minutes or until egg is fully cooked. Add meat or tofu, soy sauce and pepper to taste; stir for 1 minute more or until flavours are combined.

Makes 4 servings.

Guest Chef

Sometimes a way to get a kid to try something new is to get the "other," non-cooking parent to make it. Kids may eat Dad's chicken when they never go near Mom's; they may love Mom's pasta when they find Dad's disgusting, and they may even try Grandma's Brussels sprouts . . . well, you can hope.

Tip: Fancy it up for those with more sophisticated palates by adding 1 1/2 tsp grated gingerroot and 1 tbsp oyster sauce along with the soy sauce at the end.

NOW THIS IS GOOD

Chapter 8
Family Dinners: The Best of Times, the Worst of Times

Listen, we're parents too—we're well aware that dinner is not the best time of day. We feel lots of pressure to get healthy food—or any food for that matter—into the kids at a time when we are emotionally and physically bankrupt.

Yet here we are insisting that you try to have a family meal, and by this we mean preparing and serving only one meal to both the kids and adults at least a couple of nights a week. Kids who sit down with their families eat better overall; they are more likely to try new things and less likely to kick up a fuss. And that's just the short-term benefit. In the long term, kids who have frequent family meals acquire life skills—not only about eating, but also about the importance of connection, communication and family. These are skills that carry on through adolescence and their teen years.

If family meals are new to your family, expect some stressful times. Kids often react negatively to new experiences when there are parental expectations attached. They will squirm; they will wander; they will spill things. But just keep smiling and eating, and, as you pour yourself some vino, remind yourself that what the kids eat is not a reflection on your parenting skills. The next meal will be a little bit better. And it will get worse for a while. And then, miraculously, just when you're about to give up, your kids may actually begin to enjoy eating with you. You may never enjoy eating with them in the same way that you enjoy a romantic dinner at a fine restaurant, but if you wanted to eat filet mignon and drink Bordeaux every night, you wouldn't have had kids in the first place.

Salads, Vegetable Sides and Vegetarian Mains

Veggie Heaven

We're not sure why they call the drawer in your fridge a crisper. It's more like a vegetable morgue, where unloved greens go to get limp and soggy. So what do we do with those flaccid carrots and the morass of yellowy greens? We collect every sad veggie we have and boil the hell out of them, and then use that nutritious stock instead of water to make our kids noodles, soups, sauces and anything else we can think of.

Sesame Cucumber Salad

This light salad manages to make a boring cucumber so much more appealing. The dressing pickles the cucumber slightly, drawing the liquid out of it, so don't make it more than four hours ahead of serving or it will lose its crunch entirely.

2 tbsp	white vinegar
1 tbsp	sugar
1 tbsp	sesame oil
1 tsp	salt
1	English cucumber

Combine vinegar, sugar, sesame oil and salt in a medium bowl.

Slice cucumber thinly; add to the bowl and toss with dressing. Let sit for 30 minutes to marinate before serving.

Makes 4 servings.

Simplest Caesar Salad

This is your basic Caesar salad dressing, using a mayonnaise base instead of raw eggs, which we do for convenience as well as to avoid the "ick" factor. Plus, you can keep extra dressing around in your fridge for next week if you don't want to make a big salad tonight.

This is a relatively mild version of the classic, in deference to the child who may feel brave enough to try it, but increase the garlic or add some chopped anchovies if you desire. It's delicious with grilled chicken on top, or even a few chicken fingers or crumbled crisp bacon and croutons, sun-dried tomatoes or cold green beans.

½ cup	mayonnaise
¼ cup	olive oil (preferably a light-flavoured one)
1 tbsp	fresh lemon juice
1 tsp	finely chopped garlic
⅓ cup	freshly grated Parmesan cheese
	Salt and freshly ground pepper
2	hearts romaine lettuce, or 1 small head, washed and cut or torn into bite-size pieces

Whisk together mayonnaise, olive oil, lemon juice and garlic in a medium bowl. Add Parmesan cheese and stir to combine. Season with salt and pepper to taste.

Place lettuce in a large shallow bowl; spoon on desired amount of dressing and toss well to coat.

Makes 4 servings.

Salad Days

Some kids actually eat salad. And after heavy research in the playground, we found out why. It's all about the dressing—sweet, tangy and a little bit goopy. Caesar, ranch and honey Dijon are all kid favourites.

Confetti Power Slaw

We all know raw veggies are good for us, but the question is, how do you get your picky eater to try them? This slaw just might entice your children to try "salad" for a change. It's very colourful, plus beets make your poop turn red, and kids think that is really cool.

Think Ahead

Pre-slicing veggies and freezing them means they will always be ready for a quick stir-fry or side dish. The bags of fresh washed and sliced veggies from the produce section of the grocery store are also a great quick fix. We especially like the broccoli slaw for a quick sauté.

Tip: If you are making this ahead of time, keep the beets separate until just before serving. Otherwise, the entire salad will turn purply-red.

1 cup	grated peeled beets
1 cup	grated carrot
1	Granny Smith apple, cored and grated
2 cups	thinly sliced cabbage
1/4 cup	mayonnaise
1 tbsp	cider vinegar
1 tbsp	liquid honey
1 tbsp	lemon juice
	Salt and freshly ground pepper
2 tbsp	chopped fresh mint (optional)

Combine beets, carrots, apple and cabbage in a large bowl.

Whisk together mayonnaise, vinegar, honey and lemon juice; season with salt and pepper to taste.

Toss slaw with dressing and serve with mint on the side.

Makes 4 servings.

Indulgent Mashed Potatoes

Try as we might, we just can't rationalize using enough cream to make truly indulgent restaurant-style mashed potatoes. So our compromise is half buttermilk (which is naturally low in fat) and half cream. You can add milk instead of the cream but the potatoes might be a little thin—and that is really a sad thing for a mashed potato to be.

2 lb	Yukon gold potatoes, peeled or scrubbed, cut into 2-inch chunks
Pinch	Salt
1/4 cup	unsalted butter
1/4 cup	whipping cream
1/2–1/4 cup	buttermilk

Place potatoes in a large pot with enough cold water to cover. Add a pinch or two of salt and bring to a boil; boil for 12 to 15 minutes or until potatoes are tender. Drain water; put pot with potatoes back on the burner on low heat for 1 minute to evaporate excess water on the potatoes. Remove from heat.

Place butter and whipping cream in a small pot and heat until butter has melted. Reserve.

Mash potatoes in pot with a potato masher (or use a ricer if you have one), stir in warm butter mixture and buttermilk to taste. Season well with salt.

Makes 4 servings.

Garlic-Roasted Carrots

Simple, quick and delicious, these were a big hit with our testers. You just have to get the kids to try these once and it will be a side dish for life. And if not, more for you.

1 tbsp	unsalted butter
1 lb	carrots, peeled and cut on an angle into 1-inch pieces
2	cloves garlic, sliced
	Salt and freshly ground pepper

Melt butter in a small pot over medium heat. Add carrots and garlic; cover pot and turn down heat to medium-low. Cook, shaking pot occasionally, for 15 minutes or until carrots are tender and both carrots and garlic are slightly caramelized. Season with salt and pepper to taste.

Makes 4 servings.

Green Beans with Pecans and Brown Butter

This delicious side dish had been gracing Eshun's Thanksgiving table for years and then ping! The light went on as she realized that if her family liked it once a year, they would like it all year long. The brown butter and pecans elevate this way beyond normal dinner fare with almost no extra effort. Max picks out the pecans but eats the beans with his fingers, licking off the butter as he goes.

Running for Beans

Emma was shocked when Zachary started eating green beans after Michael, his Sportplay coach, told him *never* to eat green beans because they would make him run too fast. (To be honest, Emma always thought Zachary was too smart to fall for such obvious reverse psychology.) He now happily gobbles up green (and yellow and purple) beans, boasting how this week he will win the sprint.

10 oz	green beans, stem ends removed and halved
1 tbsp	unsalted butter
¼ cup	pecan halves
	Salt
1 tsp	chopped fresh parsley (optional)

Bring a large pot of salted water to a boil. Add beans; blanch for 3 minutes or until tender-crisp. Drain.

Heat butter in a frying pan over medium-low heat until it begins to turn golden, 2 to 3 minutes. Add pecans, stirring to coat in butter; sauté for 2 minutes or until fragrant and toasted. Add blanched beans to pan and toss to coat in butter. Season with salt to taste and sprinkle with parsley (if using).

Makes 4 servings.

Quick Dark Greens Sauté

We both get boxes of organic fruits and vegetables delivered weekly to our door, and while we use different companies, we find we often end up with large bunches of Swiss chard, kale or collard greens that we probably would not have purchased on our own. That being said, we know these greens are VERY good for us. Here's a quick and tasty way to cook them so they don't wither away at the back of the veggie drawer. The balsamic vinegar adds a sweetness that tames the strong flavour of the greens.

1	bunch Swiss chard, kale or collard greens, well washed, tough centre ribs removed, torn or cut into bite-size pieces
2 tbsp	olive oil
1 tbsp	chopped garlic
Pinch	hot pepper flakes
2 tsp	balsamic vinegar
	Salt and freshly ground pepper

Place prepared greens in a steamer; cover and steam over boiling water for 3 to 5 minutes or until tender. Remove from heat and reserve, uncovered.

Heat olive oil in a wok or frying pan over medium-high heat. Add garlic and hot pepper flakes; sauté for 30 seconds or until golden. Add cooked greens; stir-fry for 1 minute, tossing greens in hot oil to coat. Add balsamic vinegar; cook, tossing, for 1 minute more. Season with salt and pepper to taste.

Makes 4 servings.

Other Uses for Greens

- Use them instead of spinach in soups.
- Deep-fry shredded kale until crisp.
- For a Southern treat, cook collard greens with chicken stock, a pinch of brown sugar and a smoked turkey or ham bone for 90 minutes or until melt-in-your-mouth tender.
- Combine kale, potatoes and leftover sausage with chicken or vegetable stock for a Portuguese-style soup.

Tip: The ribs of Swiss chard are very tasty. Cut them as you would celery and stir-fry them with the garlic and hot pepper flakes until tender before adding the cooked leaves.

Spiced Oven Home Fries

Are there any kids out there who will reject french fries? We think not. And with a little bit of work, you can convince your family that these "home fries" are just as good if not better than the ones you grab from the drive-through—well, a good substitute, since you are not going to invest in a deep-fryer.

The curry paste gives the potatoes a boost without making them taste "curried," but you could substitute 1 tbsp dried Italian seasoning if you prefer, or just leave them plain. If you want to make the potatoes look more like "real" fries, cut them into $\frac{1}{2}$-inch sticks and turn them after about 15 minutes so they'll be evenly golden.

2 lb	Yukon Gold potatoes, peeled or scrubbed, cut into 1-inch chunks
2 tbsp	olive oil
1 tbsp	Madras or mild curry paste
	Salt

Preheat oven to 450°F.

Combine olive oil and curry paste in a bowl; add potatoes and toss to coat. Season well with salt to taste.

Place potatoes in a single layer on a baking sheet. Bake, using a spatula to stir once, for 25 to 30 minutes or until potatoes are crisp and baked through.

Makes 4 servings.

Doggone It

No parents really feel good about feeding their kids hot dogs, and yet kids love them. There are a lot of different dogs available now, marketed to try to make you feel better about feeding them to your loved ones. The truth is that hot dogs are filled with fat, salt and nitrates, none of which are particularly healthy. Turkey and chicken dogs are slightly better, but read the nutrition labels; some of them have extra fat added to make them juicier. The best choice by far is veggie dogs, with half the fat and twice the protein. They can be eaten raw, boiled or microwaved, but definitely taste best when grilled.

Broccoli Redux

Begone, boring broccoli! These two new takes bring out broccoli's natural sweetness and add some new-fangled flavour.

Gingered Broccoli

2 tbsp	vegetable oil
2 tsp	chopped gingerroot
2 heads	broccoli, separated into florets, stalks peeled and sliced $1/4$-inch thick
1 cup	water
2 tbsp	soy sauce

Heat oil in a wok or large frying pan over medium-high heat. Add gingerroot; sauté for 1 minute or until lightly golden. Add broccoli stalks; stir-fry for 1 minute. Add broccoli florets and water; cover wok and steam for 3 to 4 minutes or until tender-crisp. Add soy sauce and toss to coat.

Makes 4 servings.

Roasted Broccoli

2 heads	broccoli, separated into florets, stalks peeled and sliced $1/4$-inch thick
2 tbsp	olive oil
	Salt and freshly ground pepper
2 tsp	fresh lemon juice
$1/4$ cup	freshly grated Parmesan cheese

Preheat oven to 400°F.

Toss broccoli with olive oil, and salt and pepper to taste; place in an ovenproof dish. Roast for 25 minutes or until broccoli is tender and slightly browned. Toss with lemon juice and Parmesan before serving.

Makes 4 servings.

Clear cutting

Noah refers to broccoli as trees. Since he was small, Emma has been getting him to turn the "trees" into "sticks." On the bright side, it means he eats broccoli; the downside means he only eats the florets and leaves the stalks littering the table.

Fresh Corn
Fritters

Two great things that taste great together: corn and pancakes. These are a perfect way to serve fresh corn at the end of the summer, when the thrill of eating it off the cob has worn a bit thin. You can even leave out the paprika and basil, sprinkle the fritters with powdered sugar and serve them for breakfast. These make a great side dish to barbecued, roasted or pan-fried meats of any sort, and are particularly nice served with a salad for a light meal.

1 cup	all-purpose flour
1 tsp	baking powder
1 tsp	salt
$\frac{1}{2}$ tsp	sugar
$\frac{1}{2}$–1 tsp	paprika (regular or smoked)
2	large eggs
$\frac{2}{3}$ cup	milk
3 cups	corn kernels
	(from about 4 ears of corn)
1–2 tbsp	chopped fresh basil
	Olive oil for frying

Preheat oven to 200°F.

Combine flour, baking powder, salt, sugar and paprika in a large bowl; stir with a fork. Add eggs. Pour milk over eggs; stir until batter is just uniform. Stir in corn and basil.

Heat 2 tbsp olive oil in a large heavy-bottomed frying pan over medium heat.

Using a $\frac{1}{4}$-cup measure, ladle batter into the hot oil, making 3 or 4 fritters per batch, depending on the size of your frying pan. Cook for 2 minutes per side or until fritters are golden and batter is cooked through. Place fritters on a paper towel–lined baking sheet in the oven to keep warm, while you fry the rest of the fritters.

Makes 12 fritters.

Tip: Yes, you can use frozen corn kernels—the end result isn't quite as delicious, but your kids won't know the difference. You could also try other kinds of veggies, like grated zucchini or carrot, for multi-coloured fritters.

Crisp Roasted Squash Wedges

Squash is one of those vegetables kids would like if they would only give it a chance. And this is one of the fastest and most flavourful ways we've found to cook it. Not that there's anything wrong with roasting a halved squash and mashing it up with plenty of butter, salt and pepper, but roasted this way, the sugars in the squash caramelize and give a lot of flavour for little effort (and for Max, who loves things slightly burnt, there are plenty of crispy edges). Leave the peels on and you can eat them like slices of melon, discarding the rind as you go—kind of like watermelon from the oven.

1	acorn squash, halved, seeds removed and cut into wedges 1 inch thick at base
1 tbsp	olive oil
	Salt and freshly ground pepper

Preheat oven to 450°F.

Place squash wedges in a large bowl. Drizzle with olive oil and season with salt and pepper to taste; toss to coat. Lay squash in a single layer on a baking sheet; roast for 30 to 35 minutes, turning halfway through baking, or until evenly browned and very tender.

Makes 4 servings.

Roasted Root Vegetables

Kids love potatoes, but turnips? Parsnips? The funny thing is, these other vegetables in the root family are actually sweeter than potatoes, especially when roasted. So try to sell them on the candy factor.

1	large white turnip (about 10 oz), peeled and cut into 1/2-inch dice
1 lb	parsnips (3–4), peeled and cut into 1/2-inch dice
2 tbsp	olive oil
1 tbsp	chopped garlic
2 tsp	sugar
	Salt and freshly ground pepper
3	sprigs fresh thyme

Preheat oven to 425°F.

Combine turnip and parsnips in a large bowl. Toss with olive oil, garlic, sugar, and salt and pepper to taste. Place in a 9- x 13-inch baking dish and tuck in thyme sprigs.

Roast vegetables, stirring occasionally, for 40 to 45 minutes or until tender and browned. Discard thyme before the children see it, and serve.

Makes 4 to 6 servings.

Curried Lentils

We are strongly encouraging you, almost begging you, to try to work lentils into your diet. Not just because they are healthy, but also because they are delicious. A good first step in the lentil rehabilitation program is boiling them up and mixing them with rice. Or go for this recipe because it is fragrant and exotic and tastes great cold the next day.

Tip: Du Puy lentils are small French greenish brown lentils that hold their shape during cooking, although they do take longer to cook. The more common brown lentil can get mushy if overcooked. The Indian red lentil has had its shell removed and is supposed to get mushy—it's the one used for the Indian dish dal.

Tip: Indian curry pastes are a good addition to the pantry as they make curries in a flash and can be spread on steaks and chicken for extra kick. Look for jars in most supermarkets. We love the flavourful Madras paste, which is somewhere in the middle between mild and hot, but use whatever heat level your family will tolerate.

1 cup	du Puy lentils or brown
2 cups	water
1 tbsp	unsalted butter
½ cup	chopped onion
2 tsp	finely chopped gingerroot
2 tsp	curry paste
½ cup	chopped tomato (canned or fresh)
½ cup	coconut milk
	Salt and freshly ground pepper

Place lentils and water in a medium pot; bring to a boil. Turn down heat to medium and simmer for 15 minutes or until lentils are tender but not fully cooked. Set aside.

Meanwhile, heat butter in a large, heavy-bottomed pot over medium heat. Add onions; sauté for 10 minutes or until golden. Add gingerroot and curry paste; sauté for 1 minute more. Add tomato; cook for 2 minutes or until flavours have begun to come together. Add coconut milk and bring to a boil. Add lentils with their cooking water; simmer for 10 minutes more or until lentils are fully cooked but have not burst and liquid has reduced to a sauce. Season with salt and pepper to taste.

Makes 4 servings.

Italian Skillet Beans

This is a simple and very satisfying vegetarian main dish. Serve over polenta or with good crusty bread. Yes, there is spinach in it. If you leave the leaves whole, they are very easy to pick out for those who won't eat it, and the rest of you can enjoy the flavour and nutrients it provides.

2 tbsp	olive oil
1 cup	chopped onions
1 tbsp	chopped garlic
1/4–1/2 tsp	hot pepper flakes
1 1/2 cups	canned Italian plum tomatoes, squished up with their juices
2	19-oz (540 mL) cans cannellini beans, drained and well rinsed
1/2 cup	vegetable or chicken stock, or water
1 tsp	chopped fresh rosemary
1 tsp	chopped fresh sage
	Salt and freshly ground pepper
1	bunch fresh spinach (6–8 cups), well washed, tough stems removed

Heat oil in a large frying pan over medium heat. Add onions; sauté for 2 minutes or until softened. Add garlic and hot pepper flakes; sauté for 1 minute more.

Add tomatoes; simmer for 2 minutes or until juices have reduced slightly.

Add beans, stock or water, rosemary and sage; simmer for 5 minutes or until flavours have come together and juices have thickened. Season with salt and pepper to taste.

Add spinach and cook, stirring, until just wilted.

Makes 4 servings.

Spinach Pie

Emma lives in the Greek area of Toronto, where almost every child eats spinach pie (spanakopita) on a regular basis. Zachary and Noah eat it several times a week, even though they will not touch spinach in any other form, and for many years it was Zachary's most complete meal.

Hide and Seek

Our friend Charlie is the queen of hide-and-seek. She does it with complete abandon and her kids don't seem to notice. An entire sweet potato or a can of puréed pumpkin into muffins, no problem. She puts miscellaneous veggies and tuna into patties, wraps chickpeas in phyllo and adds spinach to anything without batting an eye. And the kids eat it all up without a peep.

1 ½ lb	baby spinach, or spinach, well washed, with stems and centre ribs removed (6L)
⅓ cup	olive oil
2 cups	chopped onion
½ cup	chopped green onions
½ cup	crumbled feta cheese
¼ cup	freshly grated Parmesan cheese
¼ cup	chopped fresh parsley
	Salt and freshly ground pepper
3	large eggs
8	sheets phyllo pastry

Preheat oven to 375°F.

Lightly oil a 10- x 14-inch baking sheet.

Heat a large frying pan or wok over medium heat. Working in batches, add spinach to pan and cook over medium heat, stirring, for 2 minutes or until spinach has wilted. Remove spinach to a colander and let cool slightly. Repeat until all spinach is cooked. When spinach is cool enough to handle, press down on it to squeeze out liquid, then chop coarsely.

Heat 2 tbsp of the olive oil in a large frying pan over medium heat. Add onions; sauté for 5 minutes or until soft and lightly golden. Add green onions; sauté for 1 minute or until wilted. Add cooked spinach, stirring to evaporate excess moisture. Scrape spinach mixture into a large bowl and reserve.

Add feta, Parmesan and parsley to spinach mixture and toss to combine. Season with salt and pepper to taste. Beat eggs in a small bowl and season well with salt and pepper. Add eggs to spinach mixture and stir to combine.

Lay one sheet of phyllo pastry on the counter; brush lightly with olive oil. Top with another sheet of phyllo pastry and brush with oil. Repeat until you have used 4 sheets. Cover with a damp tea towel and make another identical stack of phyllo pastry.

Place one phyllo stack on a prepared baking sheet. Spread spinach mixture on phyllo base in an even layer about $\frac{1}{2}$ inch thick, leaving about 1 $\frac{1}{2}$-inch border around filling. Fold edges of pastry up and over filling; brush sides and top edge with olive oil. Centre second phyllo stack over top of spinach mixture and tuck edges underneath bottom of pie. Brush the whole pie with olive oil.

Place pie on lowest rack of oven. Bake for 40 minutes or until pastry is golden brown.

Makes 4 to 6 servings.

All Parsley Is Italian

In our opinion, curly parsley is not an edible product and is only good for decorating an equally inedible airline meal. Italian, or flat-leaf parsley actually tastes good. Your kids will not eat either form.

Starchy Sides, Pasta and Noodles

Beginner's Brown Rice

Just imagine how good you'd feel if your kids ate brown rice instead of white. We call this Beginner's Brown Rice because while we all know that brown rice is better for us than white, we also know it takes about three times longer to cook and requires some getting used to. Brown rice is a little chewier and has a slightly nutty flavour, which may appeal to your kids. We have found a way to shorten the cooking time (as long as you're able to plan ahead). Adding sesame oil plays up the rice's nuttiness.

1 cup	brown rice
2 cups	water
2 tsp	sesame oil
1 tsp	salt
1/4 cup	chopped green onions (optional)

Combine rice and water in a medium pot and let sit overnight or all day. This cuts the cooking time pretty much in half.

When ready to cook, place the pot on the stove and add sesame oil and salt; bring to a simmer. Cover and cook over low heat for 30 minutes or until water has been absorbed and rice is cooked through. Remove from heat and let sit for 5 minutes longer. Fluff with a fork. Sprinkle with green onions (if desired) and serve.

Makes about 2 1/2 cups.

Tip: We're told that brown rice retains its nutrients better and keeps from going rancid if kept in the freezer, so if you have space for a bag of it, chuck it in!

Cool Couscous Salad

Couscous is really just pasta by another name, except it's very good cold. This salad is the closest thing to a pasta salad you'll find in this book, because we don't really like cold pasta with dressing. We were floored when our kids actually ate this. Maybe it's because of all the dried fruit and bright, citrusy taste. Perhaps that's also why it's a great hit at potlucks and brunch.

1 cup	orange juice
$\frac{1}{2}$ cup	water
2 tbsp	olive oil
2 tbsp	red wine vinegar
2 tsp	grated gingerroot
1 cup	couscous
$\frac{1}{3}$ cup	chopped dried apricots
$\frac{1}{4}$ cup	dried cranberries
1 tbsp	golden raisins
	Salt

Combine orange juice, water, 1 tbsp of the oil, vinegar and gingerroot in a small pot; bring just to a boil. Set aside.

Heat remaining 1 tbsp oil in a large frying pan over medium heat. Add couscous; cook, stirring, for about 4 minutes or until it turns golden. Pour the reserved hot liquid into the frying pan over couscous; add dried cranberries and raisins. Let it boil briefly, then turn off heat. Using a fork, fluff up couscous to get rid of any lumps. Season with salt to taste.

Add an additional splash of vinegar and oil before serving. Serve at room temperature.

Makes 4 servings.

Baby Steps

If you're feeling in a rut, try expanding your kids' repertoire by starting with what you *know* they like and switching it up a bit. For example, if your kids like:

- Pasta—try couscous, and if they like couscous, try barley and quinoa.
- Pizza—try lasagna, pizza bagels.
- Chicken fingers—try fish fingers and then fried calamari.
- Spaghetti—try spaghetti squash.
- Rice—try fried rice, sticky rice.
- Shrimp—try lobster, crab cakes, scallops.
- Peas—try edamame, sugar snap peas, snow peas.

Warm Soba Noodle Salad

Soba noodles, which are made from buckwheat, are love at first bite. Brown noodles with flavour! (And without the grittiness or gumminess that so many whole wheat pastas have.) A slurping contest is a fine way to introduce new noodles into your family's diet. Who can be the noisiest? Dad wins at Emma's house, by a long shot.

½ cup	water
¼ cup	soy sauce
1 tbsp	seasoned rice wine vinegar
1 tbsp	liquid honey
¼ tsp	Asian chili sauce
8 oz	dry soba noodles
½ cup	julienned green onions
2 cups	julienned carrots
2 tbsp	black sesame seeds or toasted sesame seeds

Combine water, soy sauce, vinegar, honey and chili sauce in a small pot; bring to a boil, stirring to dissolve honey. Remove from heat.

Bring a large pot of salted water to a boil; cook soba noodles for 2 to 3 minutes or until al dente. Drain.

Toss noodles with dressing, green onions and carrots. Noodles may seem wet at first, but they will absorb the sauce. Sprinkle with sesame seeds or serve on the side if desired. Serve warm or at room temperature.

Makes 4 servings.

Ritualize It

Kids are built for rituals— that's why they fall so easily into habitual food patterns. But one ritual worth encouraging is the special weekly family meal. It can be tied to religion, or it can be a regular old Tuesday or a Sunday breakfast. Choose what works best for your family. But one night a week, pull out the tablecloth and candles and start making some family traditions. That's what good eating and good memory making are all about.

Cornbread

Cornbread is a quick and delicious addition to a soupy or saucy dinner such as chili. It is best eaten warm from the oven although leftovers are great toasted. And when you aren't sure if your kids will eat the rest of the meal, it's a great main course for them.

If you want it to be really authentic, you should make your cornbread in a cast iron frying pan (ideally a 9-inch pan), but if you don't have one, use an 8-inch square baking pan. Try it plain or mix in some of the optional additions.

1 cup	cornmeal (the coarser the better)
1 cup	all-purpose flour
2 tbsp	sugar
1 tsp	baking powder
1 tsp	salt
½ tsp	baking soda
½ tsp	chili powder
2	large eggs
1 cup	buttermilk
1 cup	grated white Cheddar cheese (optional)
1 cup	cooked fresh or defrosted frozen corn kernels (optional)
¼ cup	chopped green onions (optional)
¼ cup	unsalted butter

Preheat oven to 425°F.

Combine cornmeal, flour, sugar, baking powder, salt, baking soda and chili powder in a small bowl; stir with a fork to blend. Set aside.

Beat eggs lightly in a large bowl; add buttermilk and stir until uniform. Add flour mixture to egg mixture and stir until just combined. Stir in Cheddar cheese, corn and green onions (if using).

Melt butter in a cast iron frying pan over medium heat; remove from heat and swirl butter around to coat pan. Pour remaining melted butter into batter and stir until just incorporated.

Spoon batter into prepared frying pan; bake for 25 minutes or until set and lightly golden. Cut into wedges to serve.

Makes 4 to 6 servings.

Gougères

You didn't know that you were looking for a gougères recipe, did you? Emma had no idea what Eshun was talking about, but now she's a convert. Gougères are essentially savoury cream puffs without the filling. They sound intimidating but are pretty easy to make and add a special touch to any meal. The best part is that they are made from ingredients you probably have in your kitchen right now, and they add a hit of protein to a light meal of soup or salad.

You can use a piping bag and make lots of small perfect ones for guests, but for casual family meals, we just use a soup spoon to scoop the batter onto a baking sheet. If your children are afraid of cheese, use a mild white Cheddar, and don't sprinkle any on top.

1 cup	milk
1/3 cup	unsalted butter, cut into cubes
1/2 tsp	salt
1 1/4 cups	all-purpose flour
5	large eggs
1 cup	grated Gruyère or other hard cheese

Preheat oven to 425°F.

Combine milk, butter and salt in a medium pot over medium heat; cook until milk is warm and butter is melted. Turn heat to high and bring to a boil. Immediately remove pot from heat; add flour and stir vigorously until mixture is smooth and pulls away from the sides of the pot. Reduce heat to low. Return the pot to the stove and beat for another 30 seconds or until dough has formed a smooth ball. Remove from heat and let cool for a few minutes.

Beat 4 of the eggs into dough, one at a time, beating well to incorporate before adding the next one (this requires a little muscle). The resulting dough should be shiny and soft. Stir in 1/2 cup of the cheese. Use a soup spoon to scoop batter onto a parchment-lined baking sheet, making 8 to 10 mounds, each 2 inches in diameter. Beat remaining egg and brush over top of gougères. Sprinkle tops with remaining 1/2 cup cheese.

Bake for 20 minutes or until gougères are brown, crisp and cracked. Turn down oven temperature to 350°F and bake for another 10 minutes to dry them out so they don't collapse when removed from oven (although if they do, they will still be delicious).

Makes 4 to 6 servings.

Green Pea Risotto

If your kids like rice, they're probably going to like risotto. Fennel adds an elegant note to this otherwise straightforward risotto, and since it's white, your kids will hardly know it's there. The sweetness of the peas combined with the rich saltiness of Parmesan and butter makes this sinfully good. Throw in some cooked chicken and you have a one-pot dish.

5 cups	chicken stock (homemade or low-sodium)
2 tbsp	olive oil
2 tbsp	unsalted butter
1 cup	finely chopped fennel bulb
1 cup	finely chopped onion
1 cup	arborio or carnaroli rice
2 cups	shelled fresh or frozen peas (partially defrosted)
	Salt and freshly ground pepper
1/3 cup	freshly grated Parmesan cheese
1/4 cup	chopped fresh parsley

Heat chicken stock in a medium pot over medium heat and keep warm on low heat.

Heat olive oil and 1 tbsp of the butter in a large pot or Dutch oven over medium heat. Add fennel and onions; sauté for 5 minutes or until tender. Add rice; sauté, stirring, for 1 minute more or until rice is coated with oil.

Begin adding warm stock, about 1 cup at a time, and cook, stirring frequently, so that the rice doesn't stick to the bottom of the pot. Continue stirring until most of the stock has been absorbed. Continue adding stock to rice in this way until it has cooked for about 20 minutes in total or until you have used up most or all of the stock and the rice is almost cooked through.

Add peas and simmer for 2 minutes longer or until they are cooked through. When both rice and peas are cooked, remove pot from heat. Stir in remaining butter and cheese. Season with salt and pepper to taste.

Stir in parsley or serve on the side.

Makes 4 servings.

Pad Thai

Kids must instinctively know that there is ketchup in pad Thai, because almost all kids like it, and since parents think it tastes great, why argue? Like most noodle dishes, this is best eaten straight from the wok. Which is why, with a little practice, your noodles will taste much better than those from your favourite Thai takeout place. Traditionally, pad Thai contains chicken, tofu and shrimp, but if no one in your house likes tofu or shrimp, or if you're sick of chicken, leave it out and add more of the protein that appeals to you.

8 oz	medium-wide rice noodles
2 tbsp	sugar
2 tbsp	fish sauce
2 tbsp	fresh lime juice
2 tbsp	ketchup
1 tbsp	white vinegar
1 tsp	paprika
3 tbsp	vegetable oil
8 oz	large shrimp, peeled and deveined
4 oz	extra-firm tofu, cut into $\frac{1}{2}$-inch cubes (look for the kind that isn't packed in water)
2 tsp	chopped garlic
8 oz	boneless, skinless chicken breast, sliced into strips 2 inches long and $\frac{1}{4}$ inch thick (1 breast)
1	large egg, beaten
1 cup	bean sprouts
$\frac{1}{4}$ cup	green onions, cut into 1-inch pieces
$\frac{1}{4}$ cup	chopped dry-roasted peanuts
$\frac{1}{4}$ cup	fresh coriander leaves

Ketchup Cliché

Why isn't ketchup vitamin fortified? Then we would know our kids were getting a complete meal.

Cut It Out

Scissors are a cook's best tool. They can be used for cutting up chicken, canned tomatoes, extra-long noodles, fresh herbs and just about everything else. Just make sure you wash them before using them to cut paper. The blades can get pretty gross after a hard day's work.

(see over)

Place noodles in a large bowl and cover with hot water. Let sit for 15 minutes or until flexible but still firm. Drain, rinse with cold water, drain again and set aside.

Combine sugar, fish sauce, lime juice, ketchup, vinegar and paprika in a small bowl. Reserve.

Heat a wok over high heat until it begins to smoke. Add 1 tbsp of the oil and carefully swirl to coat pan; stir-fry shrimp for 1 to 2 minutes or until pink and just cooked through. Remove shrimp and reserve.

Add remaining 2 tbsp oil to wok and add tofu; stir-fry for 2 minutes or until pale golden. Add garlic and chicken; stir-fry for 2 minutes or until just cooked.

Push chicken and tofu to the side of the wok; add egg, lightly scrambling for 30 seconds or until half cooked. Add drained noodles; stir-fry, tossing well to combine with the other ingredients in the wok, for 1 minute or until noodles are al dente. Add reserved seasoning sauce and stir to combine.

Return shrimp to the wok along with bean sprouts and green onions; stir-fry for 1 minute longer or until shrimp are warm and bean sprouts are slightly softened. Sprinkle with peanuts and coriander leaves to serve.

Makes 4 servings.

Shake It Up

Feel like the whole family meal thing is in a rut? Shake it up a bit. Have a picnic—inside or out; try family movie night and eat a related meal in front of the TV; have a buffet; pick a country and have a theme night complete with decorations, maps and menu; have dessert first; try breakfast for dinner; have a green-eggs-and-ham lunch; let the kids cook (and then order takeout after they're in bed). Use your imagination and anything goes. You *and* the kids will have a blast—it will be so worth the little extra planning.

Spaghetti with Tuna, Tomatoes and Olives

Fridge empty? Don't despair—you probably have all these ingredients hiding in your cupboards somewhere, and other than the tomatoes you can pretty much wing it. Substitute leftover roast turkey or chicken for the tuna.

2 tbsp	olive oil
1 cup	chopped onion
1 tbsp	chopped garlic
1/8 tsp	cayenne pepper or hot smoked paprika
1	28-oz can (828 mL) Italian plum tomatoes, squished up with their juices
2 tbsp	red wine vinegar
1/4 cup	chopped pitted black olives
1	6-oz can (170 g) solid white tuna, drained, broken into chunks
	Salt and freshly ground pepper
1 lb	spaghetti or linguine
2 tbsp	chopped fresh parsley (optional)

Heat olive oil in a large frying pan over medium heat. Add onions; sauté for 2 minutes or until softened. Add garlic; sauté for 1 minute or until pale golden. Add cayenne or paprika; stir to coat onion and garlic. Add tomatoes with their juices. Bring sauce to a simmer; cook gently for 10 minutes or until flavours have blended. Stir in red wine vinegar, olives and tuna; simmer for 5 minutes longer. Season with salt and pepper to taste.

Meanwhile, bring a large pot of salted water to a boil; cook pasta according to package directions or until al dente. Drain.

Toss pasta with sauce. Sprinkle with parsley (if using) and serve.

Makes 4 servings

Tip: Long noodles like spaghetti and linguine do not hold chunky sauces very well, and in our families this proves to be something of an advantage. Once you've tossed the pasta with the sauce, all the good bits will fall to the bottom. As long as you serve your pickiest family member the from the top of the bowl, they will get relatively plain tomato sauce pasta, leaving the parents to scoop up all the good stuff from the bottom.

Farfalle with Bacon and Broccoli

Let's face it—bacon makes everything taste better. Members of our families (you know who you are) who do not officially eat red meat consider bacon a condiment and will eat it in any form. At Emma's house, this is called bacon and egg pasta because she likes to beat an egg and stir it into the hot sauce at the end.

Tip: Frozen, peeled edamame or peas are great substitutes for the broccoli in this pasta sauce.

Tip: The trick here is to use good-quality chicken stock. Homemade chicken stock thickens better and doesn't become salty when you reduce it. If you don't have any stock in your freezer, make sure you buy one that's low in sodium and doesn't contain MSG. Look for stock in Tetra Paks, as small containers of refrigerated concentrate, or even frozen, instead of canned stock.

6	slices bacon
2 tbsp	olive oil
2 cups	chopped onion
1 tbsp	chopped garlic
$\frac{1}{4}$–$\frac{1}{2}$ tsp	hot pepper flakes
2 cups	chicken stock (homemade or low-sodium)
	Salt and freshly ground pepper
1 lb	farfalle or other medium-size pasta
4 cups	broccoli florets and peeled, sliced stalks
$\frac{1}{4}$ cup	freshly grated Parmesan cheese
1 tbsp	chopped fresh parsley

Cook bacon in a large frying pan over medium heat for 8 minutes or until crisp. Remove bacon from pan and drain on a paper towel. When it has cooled, crumble into small pieces. Set aside.

Drain all but 1 tbsp fat from the pan; add olive oil and heat over medium heat. Add onions to pan; sauté for 10 minutes or until golden and very soft, stirring to incorporate any bacon bits that may be stuck to the pan. Add garlic and hot pepper flakes; sauté for 1 minute more. Add stock; bring to a boil and simmer for 12 minutes or until reduced by about ⅔ and slightly thickened. Season with salt and pepper to taste.

Meanwhile, bring a large pot of salted water to a boil; add pasta. Three minutes before pasta reaches cooking time recommended on package, add broccoli to the pot and cook for remaining time. When both the pasta and broccoli are al dente, drain; toss pasta and broccoli with sauce. Stir in Parmesan, reserved bacon and parsley (if your children do not fear small green bits). Adjust seasoning if necessary.

Makes 4 servings.

Edamame: The Super Bean

Edamame are those addictive green pods at Japanese restaurants. They pack protein, calcium, iron, fibre and phyto-chemicals, so they're like a fun-to-eat multivitamin in a pod. Edamame are soybeans, available fresh in season or frozen, shelled or in the pod. They can be found at Asian food markets, many grocery stores and health food stores. Our kids love them; the added bonus is they pop right out of the shell like a natural pea shooter. And they couldn't be easier to make: boil them for 4 minutes in water on the stove, or pop them in the microwave with a small amount of water for 2 minutes. Even if that's the only thing they eat all day, you can still feel like a good parent!

Fusilli with Roasted Eggplant and Cherry Tomatoes

Raw eggplants are beautiful. Rory used to love holding one while Eshun did the grocery shopping, but eat it? NO WAY. Roasted eggplant is delicious and makes a soft, rich and slightly smoky addition to a pasta sauce. Your kids don't need to know. You can tell them what's in the sauce after they can't live without it.

1	medium eggplant, unpeeled
1/4 cup	olive oil
	Salt and freshly ground pepper
1 lb	fusilli or other short pasta
2 cups	chopped onion
1 tbsp	chopped garlic
1 1/2 cups	chicken stock (homemade or low-sodium)
1 1/2 cups	cherry tomatoes, halved, or quartered if large
2 tsp	balsamic vinegar
1/4 cup	whole basil leaves
	Freshly grated Parmesan cheese

Preheat oven to 450°F.

Slice eggplant into 1/4-inch-thick rounds. Toss with 2 tbsp of the olive oil and season with salt and pepper. Place eggplant slices in a single layer on a baking sheet; roast for 30 minutes or until soft and browned. Chop eggplant and set aside.

Bring a large pot of salted water to a boil; cook pasta according to package directions until al dente.

Meanwhile, heat remaining 2 tbsp oil in a frying pan over medium-low heat. Add onions; sauté for 10 minutes or until golden and very soft.

Add garlic; sauté for 1 to 2 minutes or until fragrant. Add chicken stock; bring to a boil and reduce for 2 minutes or until slightly thickened. Turn up heat to medium and add tomatoes, chopped eggplant and balsamic vinegar; cook until flavours are blended. Season with salt and pepper to taste. Add basil leaves to sauce to wilt them slightly, then toss sauce with pasta. Serve with Parmesan cheese.

Makes 4 servings.

Smoked Salmon and Asparagus Pasta

This dish is our ode to the '80s and proof that some things are worth holding on to. (Just ask Emma—she met her husband in 1984.)

Most kids like smoked salmon, but it can be served on the side. If you prefer not to use whipping cream, you could substitute ¼ cup low-fat sour cream, but stir it into the sauce at the very end so it doesn't curdle.

1 tbsp	unsalted butter
½ cup	chopped red onion
½ cup	dry vermouth or white wine
1 ½ cups	chicken stock (homemade or low-sodium)
¼ cup	whipping cream
2 tsp	grated lemon rind
	Salt and freshly ground pepper
1 cup	fresh or frozen peas
5 oz	smoked salmon, cut into 1-inch pieces
½ lb	tagliatelle, preferably the kind that comes in little nests
1 lb	asparagus, tough ends removed, cut into 1-inch pieces

Heat butter in a frying pan over medium-low heat. Add onions; sauté for 4 minutes or until soft and lightly golden. Add vermouth or white wine; turn up heat to medium and simmer for 3 minutes or until liquid is reduced by half. Add chicken stock and bring to a boil. Simmer for 10 minutes or until reduced by half and slightly thickened.

Add whipping cream and lemon rind; simmer for 2 minutes or until flavours have come together. Season sauce with salt and pepper to taste. Stir in peas; simmer for 1 minute or until just cooked. Stir in salmon just before tossing with pasta.

Meanwhile, bring a large pot of salted water to a boil. Add pasta and cook according to package directions until al dente. Three minutes before pasta is fully cooked, add asparagus to cooking water. When both pasta and asparagus are fully cooked, drain and toss with sauce.

Makes 2 to 4 servings.

Chicken, Meat and Fish

Quick Chicken Curry

All over the world kids eat curry. So become a global citizen and encourage your kids to spice it up.

This recipe has enough sauce that you can add another chicken breast if you are very hungry.

3 tbsp	vegetable oil
1 lb	boneless, skinless chicken breasts, cut into 1-inch chunks (about 2 breasts)
	Salt and freshly ground pepper
1 cup	chopped onion
1 tbsp	chopped garlic
2 tsp	chopped gingerroot
1 tbsp	Madras or mild curry paste
1 cup	chopped tomatoes (canned or fresh)
½ cup	chicken stock (homemade or low-sodium)
2 tbsp	plain yogurt
2 tbsp	chopped fresh coriander

Heat 2 tbsp of the oil in a large nonstick frying pan over medium-high heat. Season chicken with salt and pepper. Add chicken to pan; sauté for 3 to 4 minutes or until lightly golden and almost cooked through. Remove chicken from pan and reserve.

Turn heat down to medium. Add remaining 1 tbsp oil to pan; then add onions; sauté for 5 minutes or until soft and lightly golden. Add garlic and gingerroot; sauté for 1 minute or until fragrant. Add curry paste; stir for 1 minute or until onions are coated. Add tomatoes and chicken stock; simmer stirring and scraping bottom of pan to incorporate any spices that are stuck to pan, for 3 minutes. Season sauce with salt and pepper to taste. Add chicken; simmer for 2 minutes more or until chicken is warmed and cooked through. Remove from heat. Stir in yogurt and sprinkle with coriander (or serve on the side).

Makes 4 servings.

Yin and Yang
Five-spice Chicken

Want to add more balance to your life? Try these spiced, dark-glazed yin-yang chicken drumsticks. With all their sticky, sweet and messy appeal, they're a hit with the kids. You could throw in a breast or a couple of thighs for the grown-ups, or cut up a whole chicken, but be aware that smaller parts will cook first. You can roast this chicken or grill it on the barbecue.

2 tbsp	teriyaki sauce
3 tbsp	hoisin sauce
2 tbsp	liquid honey
2 tsp	finely chopped garlic
½ tsp	Asian chili sauce
1 tsp	five-spice powder
3 lb	chicken drumsticks or pieces

Combine teriyaki sauce, hoisin sauce, honey, Asian chili sauce, garlic and five-spice powder in a medium bowl or resealable plastic bag. Add chicken and toss to coat. Marinate for 30 minutes at room temperature, or overnight in the refrigerator.

Preheat oven to 425°F.

Line a baking sheet with foil or parchment paper.

Place chicken pieces on prepared baking sheet in a single layer; roast, basting with marinade, for 30 to 35 minutes or until cooked through.

Makes 4 servings.

Five-spice Powder

If anyone can figure out what balance really means, please contact us. But in the meantime, you can try cooking with five-spice powder. Based on the ancient philosophy of the yin and yang, five-spice powder is made of cinnamon, star anise, pepper, cloves and fennel seed. It's the secret to that distinctive sweet, salty, sour taste of many Chinese barbecue dishes.

Two-for-One
BBQ Grilled Chicken

An easy-peasy, lemon-squeezy (as our kids would say) kind of barbecue sauce. This recipe makes a generous amount of marinade so you can either put some aside to use as a salad dressing or throw in another pound of chicken breasts and have leftovers for pasta or chicken salad. Now that's flexibility!

1/4 cup	olive oil
2 tbsp	balsamic vinegar
1 tbsp	fresh lemon juice
2 tsp	Dijon mustard
1 tsp	maple syrup
2 tbsp	chopped fresh thyme (optional)
	Salt and freshly ground pepper
2 lb	boneless, skinless chicken breasts (about 4 breasts)

Combine olive oil, balsamic vinegar, lemon juice, mustard, maple syrup and thyme (if using) in a small bowl; season with salt and pepper to taste. Pour over chicken and allow to sit for 15 minutes at room temperature, or marinate for up to 1 day in the refrigerator.

Preheat a grill on medium heat; add chicken and grill for 6 to 8 minutes per side or until just cooked through and juices run clear.

Makes 4 servings.

Cheers

All kids love to do a cheers! Especially toddlers. So why limit it to drinks? Janet, mother of three, swears that it works with all things: green beans, chicken legs, anything that can be tapped together and not fall all over the floor. So, l'chaim!

Tip: Thyme tastes great in this, but as always, you can leave it out. It's mostly black by the time the chicken is cooked.

Ginger Chicken Stir-fry

This recipe went through quite a few incarnations before we hit on a mixture of veggies that the kids thought was perfect. Sugar snap peas are the secret—who knew? Serve over steamed rice or noodles.

1 lb	boneless, skinless chicken breasts (2 breasts)
1 tbsp	grated gingerroot
¼ cup	seasoned rice wine vinegar
3 tbsp	soy sauce
2 tbsp	sesame oil
2 tsp	brown sugar
¼ tsp	Asian chili sauce
1 tbsp	cornstarch
2 tbsp	vegetable oil
2 cups	sliced peeled carrots
½ cup	sliced red onion
¼ cup	water
2 cups	sugar snap peas, ends and strings removed

Tip: You can use any combination of vegetables for this stir-fry; aim for about 4 cups altogether. We also like broccoli, green beans, celery and peppers. Cook harder vegetables like broccoli first, letting them steam in the water, then add tender vegetables after.

Slice chicken against the grain into ¼-inch slices. Place in a bowl and sprinkle with grated gingerroot.

Combine vinegar, soy sauce, sesame oil, brown sugar and chili sauce in a small bowl. Pour 2 tbsp of the mixture over chicken and toss to coat. Let chicken marinate at room temperature while you cut up the vegetables.

Whisk cornstarch into remaining sauce. Reserve.

Heat 1 tbsp of the vegetable oil in a wok or large nonstick frying pan over high heat. Add chicken; sauté for 2 to 3 minutes or until golden and cooked through. Remove to a plate and reserve.

Add remaining 1 tbsp oil to wok. Add carrots and onions; stir-fry for 1 minute. Add water; cover wok, and let vegetables steam for 2 minutes or until carrots are almost cooked and water has mostly evaporated. Add sugar snap peas; stir-fry for 2 minutes more or until they have turned bright green. Return chicken to wok along with remaining sauce; stir-fry for 1 minute more or until chicken is warm and sauce has thickened.

Makes 4 servings.

Parmesan Chicken Cutlets

Consider these a bridge to the wider world of chicken that does not come in kid-enticing shapes and deep-fried. You can also bake the chicken on an oiled baking sheet for 10 minutes in a 425°F oven, then broil for 3 minutes longer or until the top is browned.

4	boneless, skinless chicken breasts (about 2 lb)
	Salt and freshly ground pepper
2 tbsp	Dijon mustard
2 tsp	white wine vinegar
2 tsp	chopped garlic
1 ½ cups	fresh bread crumbs
¾ cup	freshly grated Parmesan cheese
¼ cup	vegetable oil

Slice each chicken breast horizontally and open it like a book; season with salt and pepper.

Combine mustard, vinegar and garlic; spread over chicken.

Combine bread crumbs, Parmesan and 2 tbsp of the vegetable oil on a plate. Coat chicken in crumb mixture, pressing to achieve the best coating possible, then shaking to remove any excess.

Heat remaining 2 tbsp oil in a large nonstick pan over medium heat. Working in batches, add chicken; fry for 2 minutes per side or until coating is evenly brown and chicken is cooked through.

Makes 4 servings.

Are You Chicken?

You may have noticed a trend: suddenly everything you serve is chicken—ribs are chicken, chicken is chicken, even salmon is red chicken. Kids like chicken, so go with it. They have their whole lives to figure out what chicken really looks (and tastes) like.

Provençal Chicken

Pre-marinated

Wendy, mother of Morley and Mina, buys the bulk pack–sized boneless chicken breasts. As soon as she gets home from the grocery store, she throws them into small resealable bags along with a shot of homemade or store-bought marinade. She squishes the chicken in the marinade to coat, then pops the bags into the freezer. Before work, she pulls four breasts out of the freezer, puts them into the fridge to defrost and cooks them up when she gets home.

This dish is good enough to serve to real people and can be adapted for all tastes. In Emma's house, the grown-ups eat the whole thing, Zachary gets plain chicken devoid of all sauce, and Noah gets chicken with a little bit of sauce mixed into his rice.

3 tbsp	olive oil
1 cup	all-purpose flour for dredging
	Salt and freshly ground pepper
1 lb	boneless, skinless chicken thighs (about 8)
1 cup	chopped onion
2	anchovy fillets, minced
	OR
2 tsp	Worcestershire sauce
1	19-oz (540 mL) can Italian plum tomatoes, squished up with their juice
1 tbsp	chopped garlic
½ cup	chicken stock (homemade or low sodium)
2 tsp	chopped fresh thyme
1	bay leaf
½ cup	black olives, pitted
2 tbsp	chopped fresh parsley (optional)

Heat 2 tbsp oil in a large deep frying pan or Dutch oven over medium-high heat.

Place flour in a shallow dish and season well with salt and pepper. When oil is hot, dredge chicken in flour, shaking off any excess. Working in batches, cook chicken for 2 minutes per side or until browned. Remove chicken to a plate. Reserve.

Add remaining 1 tbsp oil to pan. Turn down heat to medium and add onions and anchovies or Worcestershire; cook for 5 minutes or until onions are soft. Add garlic; cook for 1 minute longer. Add tomatoes, stock, thyme and bay leaf; bring to a gentle simmer.

Add olives and chicken. Submerge chicken in sauce and cook, turning chicken after the first 15 minutes, for 30 minutes or until cooked through.

Adjust seasonings if necessary.

If company is coming, sprinkle chicken with parsley.

Makes 4 servings.

Don't Let This Be You

Sally's son will only eat canned noodles in tomato sauce, and it has to be a cartoon shape. In their house, it's called pasta soup, and Sally hangs her head in shame. She said it was a slow decline from pasta in tomato sauce to plain pasta to the canned stuff. "We went to my in-laws once for dinner and forgot to bring the usual can. We were having a lovely roast beef dinner, and I was just praying he would eat something, anything. He looked at his plate and then said, ever so politely, 'Excuse me, Granny, but I don't eat real food. Do you have any pasta soup?'"

Turkey and Bean Chili

Our kids won't touch chili, but so many parents told us their kids love it that we thought we should include a recipe here.

The trick to good chili is simmering it for at least an hour or until the flavours have melded and the ingredients are really soft. So this won't work for most weeknights unless you have a slow cooker. You could make it a Sunday project with the kids—ideal since it gets better as it sits. And it makes your house smell delicious.

We've used ground turkey here, but you could also use ground beef, the vegetarian soy product that looks like ground meat, or even sausage if you prefer. Cornbread is, of course, the traditional accompaniment (see page 123 for the recipe).

(see page 123 for the recipe).

At Your Service

Are the kids always bugging you to get their drinks and snacks just as you sit down with the paper and a cup of coffee? Give your kids some independence—place some cups and plates in a cupboard within their reach so they can help themselves. And then have faith in them to use their power wisely.

Tip: For recipes that require lots of chopping, do it in stages. Chop up a few things when you have a bit of time in the morning and set aside. Just keep adding to the pile as the day goes on.

2 tbsp	olive oil
1 ½ cups	chopped onion
1 ½ cups	chopped celery
1 ½ cups	chopped red pepper
2 tbsp	chopped garlic
2 tsp	chili powder
1 ½ tsp	ground cumin
1 lb	ground turkey
2	28-oz (828 mL) cans Italian plum tomatoes, squished up with their juice
1	19-oz (540 mL) can Mexican red or kidney beans, drained and well rinsed
1	19-oz (540 mL) can black beans, drained and well rinsed
2 tbsp	red wine vinegar
2 tsp	dried basil
	Salt and freshly ground pepper
½ cup	grated Cheddar cheese

Heat oil over medium heat in a large, wide pot or Dutch oven. Add onions; sauté for 2 minutes or until softened. Add celery, red peppers, garlic, chili powder and cumin; sauté, stirring frequently, for 5 minutes more or until vegetables are softened.

Turn up heat to medium-high and add turkey; sauté, stirring to break meat into small pieces, for 4 minutes or until turkey is no longer pink.

Stir in tomatoes, red and black beans, vinegar and basil; bring to a boil. Turn down to a gentle simmer and cook for 1 hour or until flavours have mellowed and combined. Season with salt and pepper to taste.

Serve with grated Cheddar cheese for sprinkling on top.

Makes 4 servings.

No, Thank You

To be honest, we're not caught up in the manners thing. Perhaps because we're used to our picky eaters, our expectations have more to do with keeping our children from calling their carefully prepared dinner "disgusting" than asking us to "please pass the potatoes." But that aside, one of our pet peeves is hearing parents trying to get toddlers who can barely speak to say please and thank you. No matter how early you start, words that are not connected to real live objects do not make sense to kids until they are way over the age of two.

Chicken Pot Pie

Swanson's chicken pot pies were a staple of Eshun's childhood. The frozen standby her mother relied upon on when she couldn't face cooking was just fine with the small picky folk. But when Eshun tried them again as an adult, they weren't so tasty. So now she makes her own to satisfy the craving. Yes, the amount of work is more special-occasion fare than instant dinner, but it's so good, and you can definitely serve it to company. If you have the time, make two and stash one in the freezer.

Tip: If you don't happen to have a whole lot of cooked leftover chicken or turkey around, you can purchase a cooked rotisserie chicken from the grocery store, or follow our recipe for chicken stock (pages 64–65), which gives you a whole moist poached chicken.

⅓ cup	unsalted butter
1 cup	chopped onions
1 cup	chopped leeks, white part only
1 cup	chopped celery
2 cups	chopped carrots
2 cups	diced Yukon gold potatoes
2 cups	quartered white or brown mushrooms
⅓ cup	all-purpose flour
4 cups	chicken stock (homemade or low-sodium)
2 tbsp	whipping cream (optional)
4 cups	cooked chicken, cut or torn into bite-size pieces
1 cup	green beans or sugar snap peas, trimmed, string removed and cut into 1-inch lengths
	Salt and freshly ground pepper
½ lb	frozen puff pastry, defrosted
1	egg
1 tbsp	milk

Heat oven to 375°F.

Melt butter in a large pot or Dutch oven over medium heat. Add onions, leeks, celery and carrots; sauté for 5 minutes or until slightly softened. Add potatoes and mushrooms; sauté for 2 minutes or until mushrooms release their juices.

Add flour; stir well to coat vegetables. Cook for 2 minutes, stirring constantly to keep flour from browning. Slowly add stock to pot, stirring to dissolve flour, and bring to a boil. Turn down heat and simmer for 2 minutes or until broth has thickened. Add cream (if desired) and season with salt and pepper. Add chicken and green beans or sugar snap peas. Remove from heat and let cool to room temperature.

Spoon chicken stew into a 9- x 11-inch casserole dish or ramekins. Moisten the edge of the casserole dish with water. Roll out puff pastry to fit the size and shape of dish; place over stew. Trim or fold edges and press pastry against the casserole edge to seal. Beat together egg and milk; brush over pastry. Using a sharp knife, make a few cuts in pastry to let steam escape while baking.

Bake for 35 to 40 minutes or until pastry is golden and filling is bubbling.

Makes 6 to 8 servings.

Tip: While it is certainly easier to pull a box of puff pastry out of your freezer, secretly we prefer the doughiness of real pastry on our pot pies. If you agree it's worth the effort, you could use the recipe for the flaky pastry that tops our Deep-dish Pear and Cranberry Pie (page 170) or the Oatmeal Scone recipe (pages 90–91).

Tip: If you are baking from frozen, cover the pot pie with foil and bake at the same temperature for about two hours, uncovering after an hour to let the pastry brown.

A+ Burgers

The trick to making a better-than-average burger is adding interesting seasonings without including anything your child might want to pick out. And yes, sautéing the onions is essential to a juicy burger—have patience, you can do it. Handle the patties as little as possible, which is slightly counterintuitive since you have to mix in the ingredients—but we trust you can find the right balance.

Make small burgers—no more than three inches in diameter and less than a ½-inch thick for kids—and use a round cutter to make a mini bun from a regular bun. This is as practical as it is cute. Small hands have an easier time holding the burger, so kids will be able to get more than just bun in their mouths—and stomachs.

If you're using chicken, try to find ground dark meat—it's juicier and much more flavourful. This means there will be more moisture in the mix, so you may want to add up to ¼ cup fresh bread crumbs to make the mixture easier to shape and ensure it holds together on the barbecue.

1 tbsp	olive oil
1 cup	finely chopped onion
1 lb	ground chicken or beef
¼ cup	your favourite barbecue sauce
	Salt and freshly ground pepper

Food Subterfuge

Try adding grated veggies or cheese to:
- Soup
- Red pasta sauce
- Muffins
- Burgers/meat loaf
- Anything wrapped in phyllo
- Anything battered
- Smoothies
- Pancakes

Tip: How do you season a meat mixture to taste when you don't want to taste raw meat? After seasoning, take a little piece of the mixture and cook it briefly in a frying pan or microwave. Now that it's cooked you can safely decide whether you want to add more salt and pepper.

Heat oil in a frying pan over medium heat. Add onions; sauté for 4 minutes or until softened and lightly browned. Remove from heat and cool.

Combine meat, sautéed onions, barbecue sauce, and salt and pepper to taste in a mixing bowl; mix until just blended.

Shape mixture into patties about ¹/₂-inch thick. Chill in refrigerator until ready to cook.

Heat barbecue on high; cook burgers for 4 minutes per side or until cooked to desired degree of doneness.

Makes 4 burgers.

Thai Burger Variation:

This is a bit more work but truly delicious. Follow the recipe and method above, omitting the barbecue sauce and adding this mixture in its place: 1 tsp chopped gingerroot, ¹/₂ tsp chopped garlic, ¹/₂ tsp grated lime rind, ¹/₂ tsp fish sauce and ¹/₄ tsp Asian chili sauce.

Making the Connection

When Zachary asked what kind of animal a prosciutto was, Emma knew she was in trouble. Does she tell him it's a pig and run the risk of his abandoning a source of meat? Or tell him it's a funny animal called a prosciutto, which he has never seen before. She went with the latter. But many five-year-olds do make the connection and become vegetarians for a while because they don't want to eat Chicken Little for dinner. Just roll with it. Try to be sensitive to their views; they may be temporary. In the meantime, a few vegetarian meals never hurt anybody.

Fajitas with Guacamole, Salsa and Fixin's

Fajitas are always a hit because there is something for everyone—even your pickiest eater will probably eat a plain tortilla, maybe even with a handful of grated cheese. Put all the tasty add-ins into small bowls on the table so kids can grab what they want. Don't despair—the less they eat, the more there is for you.

During whatever you consider barbecue season, you can prepare these on your barbecue instead of in a pan: marinate the chicken breasts or steaks whole and just chop the onion and peppers in half before sticking them on the grill.

2 tbsp	olive oil
1 tbsp	fresh lime juice
2 tsp	chopped garlic
1 tsp	ground cumin
1 tsp	chili powder
	Salt and freshly ground pepper
1 lb	boneless, skinless chicken breasts (2 breasts)
	OR
	strip loin, cut into $\frac{1}{4}$-inch-thick strips
6–8	10-inch flour tortillas

Guacamole:

1	large avocado (or 2 small)
2 tsp	fresh lime juice
$\frac{1}{2}$ tsp	chopped garlic
	Salt

Salsa:

2 tbsp	chopped red onion
1 cup	chopped tomato
1 tbsp	olive oil
1 tbsp	red wine vinegar
1 tbsp	chopped coriander
	Salt

Vegetables:

1 tbsp	olive oil
1	small onion, peeled, halved and thinly sliced
1	green pepper, halved, seeded and thinly sliced
1	red pepper, halved, seeded and thinly sliced
	Salt and freshly ground pepper

Sides:

1 cup	grated Cheddar or Monterey Jack cheese
$\frac{1}{2}$ cup	sour cream

(see over)

Sometimes kids use picky eating as a way to gain attention, so try giving it to them before you sit down to a meal—have them help out in the kitchen. Yes, your cookies will have that lovely crunch of eggshell, the mac and cheese may have too much cheese on it, and the lettuce will not be as dry as you want it to be. But making kids feel they have contributed may make your mealtime a bit smoother. And they may even taste something they have made. Max first tried raw carrots after he enjoyed peeling them himself, and Noah will try a food he's helped make—but only while it's still in the pot; often he won't touch it on the plate in front of him.

Combine 1 tbsp of the olive oil, lime juice, garlic, cumin, chili powder, and salt and pepper to taste in a medium bowl. Add chicken breasts or beef and toss to coat. Allow to marinate at room temperature while you prepare the side dishes.

Heat oven to 250°F.

Wrap tortillas in foil and place in oven to warm.

Guacamole: Mash avocado with lime juice and garlic; season with salt to taste. Reserve.

Salsa: Combine red onions and tomato with olive oil, vinegar and coriander; season with salt to taste. Reserve.

Heat a large frying pan over medium-high heat. Add chicken or beef; sauté for 4 minutes or until meat is slightly browned and cooked through. Remove meat from pan and cover to keep warm.

Vegetables: Add remaining oil to pan. Add onions and green and red peppers; sauté for 5 minutes or until vegetables have softened and are slightly browned, scraping the bottom of the pan to incorporate any caramelized chicken or beef juices. Season with salt and pepper to taste.

Place chicken, vegetables, guacamole, salsa, grated cheese and sour cream in the centres of the warm tortillas. Roll up and eat.

Makes 4 servings.

Stir-fried Pork with Cashews

Here's a favourite takeout dish adapted for the home kitchen. It covers all taste sensations, the dark and slightly sweet sauce contrasting nicely with the nuts. The vegetables provide good colour and crunch and are big enough to be avoided. This recipe is equally delicious made with boneless, skinless chicken breasts. Serve over steamed rice.

1/4 cup	soy sauce
1 tbsp	dry vermouth or white wine
1 tbsp	sesame oil
1 tbsp	cornstarch
3/4 lb	pork tenderloin, cut into 1/4- x 2-inch strips
1 tbsp	sugar
1/4 tsp	Asian chili sauce
2 tbsp	vegetable oil
1 tbsp	chopped gingerroot
2 tsp	chopped garlic
1 cup	celery, cut on an angle into 1/2-inch-thick pieces
1 cup	red pepper, cut into 1-inch dice
1/4 cup	water
2	green onions, cut into 1-inch lengths
1/3 cup	roasted unsalted cashews or peanuts

Whisk together 2 tbsp of the soy sauce, vermouth, sesame oil and cornstarch in a medium bowl. Add pork; marinate for 10 minutes at room temperature. Drain off marinade, reserving pork and marinade separately.

Combine remaining 2 tbsp soy sauce, sugar and chili sauce in a small bowl. Reserve.

Heat wok or large frying pan over high heat until smoking. Add 1 tbsp of the vegetable oil and carefully swirl to coat. Add pork; stir-fry for 2 to 3 minutes or until pork is browned and just cooked through. Remove from wok and reserve.

Add remaining 1 tbsp vegetable oil along with gingerroot and garlic; stir-fry for 30 seconds. Add celery; stir-fry for 1 minute. Add red peppers; stir-fry for 1 minute more. Add water and stir to loosen any browned bits stuck to bottom of pan. Cover and steam for 1 minute or until vegetables are tender-crisp. Add green onions and nuts along with pork, remaining marinade and soy sauce mixture. Bring to a boil, stirring, for 1 minute or until sauce has thickened and pork is heated thorough. Serve immediately.

Makes 4 servings.

Beef and Chicken Satay with Peanut Dipping Sauce

It's a meat lollipop! Both adults and kids seem to enjoy food that comes with its own handle. Just beware of the mini-Zorros at your table.

These satays can be made with beef or chicken; choose one or halve the marinade and make both.

1 ½ lb	beef tenderloin, strip loin or other good grilling cut
	OR
	boneless, skinless chicken breasts or thighs
2 tbsp	soy sauce
1 tbsp	vegetable oil
1 tbsp	fresh lemon juice
1 tbsp	light brown sugar
2 tsp	chopped garlic
2 tsp	ground cumin
2 tsp	ground coriander
1 tsp	turmeric
	Peanut Dipping Sauce (recipe next page)

Trim beef or chicken of fat; slice against the grain into ¼-inch slices.

Combine soy sauce, oil, lemon juice, brown sugar, garlic, cumin, coriander and turmeric in a medium bowl. Add sliced meat and toss to coat. Cover and marinate for 1 hour at room temperature or in the refrigerator overnight.

Thread meat onto bamboo or metal skewers; grill in batches on a grill pan or barbecue over high heat for 1 to 2 minutes per side or until beef is medium-rare or chicken is just cooked through. Pass Peanut Dipping Sauce to serve.

Makes 4 servings.

Peanut Dipping Sauce

1 tbsp	vegetable oil
$\frac{1}{2}$ cup	chopped red onion
2 tsp	chopped garlic
$\frac{1}{4}$ tsp	hot pepper flakes
1 cup	coconut milk
2 tbsp	soy sauce
2 tbsp	ketchup
2 tbsp	fresh lime juice
$\frac{1}{2}$ cup	smooth natural peanut butter
2 tbsp	water (optional)
	Salt and freshly ground pepper

Heat oil in a small pot over medium heat. Add onions; sauté for 2 minutes or until softened. Add garlic and hot pepper flakes; sauté for 1 minute or until fragrant. Add coconut milk and bring to a boil; boil for 4 minutes or until reduced and thickened.

Remove from heat. Stir in soy sauce, ketchup and lime juice; allow mixture to cool to room temperature. Stir in peanut butter. If sauce begins to separate and look curdled, or if it seems too thick, whisk in water. Season with salt and pepper to taste. Serve with beef or chicken satays.

Eating Out *is* Possible

The trick to eating out with your kids is starting early. Kids who used a menu as a teething toy will be better at sitting in a restaurant than those who stayed at home until they could read the specials. We have learned:

- Asian food rules! Rice, miso soup, vegetable maki, noodles, deep-fried shrimp and even dim sum are big.
- Carry snacks. Seems counter-intuitive but snacks can stave off hunger and double as toys in an emergency.
- Take playthings. We like crayons, books, toy cars, but anything can be a toy—jam containers can be blocks and pennies are perfect for finger hockey.
- Expect some exercise. If Junior gets a bit too boisterous someone will have to sacrifice their meal and go for a walk.
- Tip big. And we mean really big.

Pork Chops with Pineapple

This '70s-influenced dish is to be blamed squarely on Eshun's mom, who has memories of a "wonderful dish of pork and pineapple from a Hawaiian cookbook." Strangely, pork and pineapple do go well together, especially when the sauce has a slightly Asian bent, and kids love it.

1 tbsp	vegetable oil
1 cup	all-purpose flour for dredging
	Salt and freshly ground pepper
4	boneless pork loin chops
	(about 1 inch thick)
1/4 cup	chopped shallots
1 tbsp	chopped gingerroot
1/2 cup	dry vermouth or white wine
1 1/2 cups	chicken stock
	(homemade or low-sodium)
1 cup	fresh or drained canned
	pineapple chunks
1 tbsp	soy sauce
1 tbsp	unsalted butter, cut into pieces

Heat oil in a frying pan over medium-high heat.

Place flour in a shallow dish and season well with salt and pepper. When oil is hot, dredge pork chops in flour mixture, shaking off excess.

Add pork chops to pan; cook for 3 minutes per side or until browned. Transfer pork to a plate and reserve.

Turn down heat to medium. Add shallots and gingerroot; sauté for 1 minute or until shallots are softened. Add vermouth and simmer for 3 minutes or until reduced to about 2 tbsp. Add chicken stock and pineapple chunks; bring to a boil. Simmer for 5 minutes or until stock has reduced and thickened slightly. Stir in soy sauce. Return pork to pan along with any accumulated juices. Cover pan and simmer over low heat for 5 minutes or until pork is cooked through. Remove lid and stir butter into sauce.

Makes 4 servings.

Meat Loaf

Maybe you think of meat loaf as an unhealthy meal from the '50s. We think of it as an opportunity to hide nutritious food in a kid-friendly hamburger-type substance. There are oatmeal, carrots, parsnips and spinach in there, or you can choose to leave all the veggies out, or put one or two more in. If your kids are hamburger fans but the words meat loaf scare them, then you know what to do.

1 lb	lean ground beef
½ lb	ground pork
1 cup	chopped onion
½ cup	grated carrot or parsnip
½ cup	chopped spinach
½ cup	large-flake oatmeal (not instant)
3 tbsp	milk
½ tsp	chopped fresh thyme
1	egg
¼ cup	ketchup
2 tbsp	Worcestershire sauce
2 tbsp	soy sauce
¼ tsp	hot pepper sauce
	Salt and freshly ground pepper
1 tsp	brown sugar

Preheat oven to 350°F.

Combine beef, pork, onions, carrot or parsnip, spinach, oatmeal, milk, thyme and egg in a large bowl.

Mix together ketchup, Worcestershire sauce, soy sauce and hot pepper sauce in a small bowl. Reserve half the sauce. Pour the other half over the meat mixture and stir gently to combine ingredients. Season meat mixture with salt and pepper to taste.

Add brown sugar to reserved sauce. Pack meat into 5- x 9-inch loaf pan and smooth top.

Bake for 30 minutes then remove meat loaf from oven. Using a knife, make 3 slits in top. Pour remaining sauce over top so that it runs into slits.

Bake for another 30 minutes. Turn on the broiler and broil for an additional 5 minutes. Pour off any fat, then carefully remove meat loaf from pan and let sit for 5 minutes before serving.

Makes 4 to 6 servings.

BBQ Ribs

At the risk of offending some vegetarians out there (including the ones we are related to), you'd have to be crazy not to like a rack of sweet, yummy ribs, and this is the simplest possible recipe for making good ones. There's nothing cuter than a little kid holding a piece of bone—a pint-sized Neanderthal.

½ cup	your favourite barbecue sauce
½ cup	beer
1	rack baby back pork ribs (about 2 lb) Salt and freshly ground pepper

Weird Combos

Kids don't live by our rules and often put funny things together and still enjoy them.

Madoc likes Cheddar cheese cubes dipped in chocolate pudding. He also likes his hot dogs with ranch dressing. Noah enjoys crackers dipped in his chocolate milk, and Maddy has her bagel with peanut butter, cream cheese, honey, mashed banana and/or jam (only the jam is optional).

Preheat oven to 350°F.

Combine barbecue sauce and beer in a small bowl. Line a roasting pan or baking dish large enough to hold ribs in a single layer with parchment paper or foil.

Remove membrane from back of ribs. Place ribs in baking dish; season with salt and pepper to taste. Pour sauce mixture over ribs, spreading it over and around the meat. Let ribs sit in pool of sauce.

Cover baking dish with foil and wrap it tightly around dish. Bake for 1 ½ to 2 hours or until ribs are very tender.

Remove ribs from baking pan (they will be grey and yucky looking). Turn up the temperature to 400°F or heat barbecue on medium. Brush sauce from bottom of pan all over ribs; roast on a baking sheet or grill for 20 minutes or until ribs are appetizingly browned. Remove from heat and let stand 5 minutes before cutting into servings.

Makes 4 servings.

Salmon Teriyaki

You already know how important fish is for kids and how it's considered "brain food," and we don't want to bore you. But just to reiterate, fish contains the all-important omega-3 oils that are good for the heart as well as the brain. Salmon does seem to be the most popular with kids. Maybe it's the cool colour.

Cooking the salmon at a high heat caramelizes the sauce slightly while creating a beautifully moist piece of fish. And the teriyaki sauce is a sweet, sticky combination that can also be used on chicken and flank steak.

¼ cup	soy sauce
2 tbsp	cider vinegar
2 tbsp	dry vermouth or white wine
1 tbsp	light brown sugar
1 tbsp	chopped gingerroot
1 tsp	chopped garlic
2 lb	salmon fillet, in 1 piece or cut into 4 pieces

Preheat oven to 450°F.

Line a baking sheet with foil.

Combine soy sauce, vinegar, vermouth, sugar, gingerroot and garlic in a small pot; bring to a boil over medium-low heat and simmer, stirring occasionally, for 6 minutes or until reduced by half and slightly thickened. Strain and cool.

Place salmon on prepared baking sheet; brush with teriyaki sauce.

Bake for 16 to 18 minutes or until salmon is just cooked through.

Makes 4 servings.

Good Taste
"Salmon tastes a bit weird, but I still like it anyway."
Rhys, age 4

Shrimp Sauté

If you haven't thought about giving your kids some shrimp for a quick and easy dinner, run to your local grocery and fry them up. Almost all grocery stores sell a house brand. We buy the frozen, peeled ones so we don't get all messy, even though we know in our heart of hearts that the unpeeled are much tastier. Kids like the unthreatening taste of shrimp, and we like that they are easy and healthy, and go well with pasta, rice or bread.

2 tbsp	olive oil
1 tsp	chopped garlic
1 lb	extra large shrimp (20–30), peeled and de-veined
⅓ cup	dry vermouth or white wine
1 tbsp	fresh lemon juice
4 tbsp	butter
	Salt and freshly ground pepper

Heat olive oil in medium frying pan over medium heat. Add chopped garlic; sauté for 1 minute. Add shrimp; cook for 3 minutes, turning once or until just cooked through. Remove shrimp from pan and cover to keep warm.

Deglaze pan with vermouth and heat until boiling for 1 minute. Turn down heat to medium-low; add lemon juice and butter. Let simmer for 2 minutes. Season with salt and pepper to taste, then pour over shrimp.

Makes 4 servings.

Tip: Shrimp is cooked when it is a "C" and overcooked when it is an "O."

Shaken, Not Stirred

In an ideal world, we would always have an open chilled bottle of white wine on hand to both drink and splash into our sauces. Sadly, it's not always true, which is why dry vermouth is a good option. Dry vermouth is quite inexpensive, will keep indefinitely in your liquor cabinet, and works so well in cooking that you may come to prefer it over white wine. And if not, you could always drink it since a good martini is nothing without it. But if you do have some dregs of white wine left over in the bottle, you can store it in a resealable bag in the freezer for cooking and just keep topping it up with the leftovers from other bottles.

East Coast Fish Cake

Remember When?

What did your parents say when you complained about dinner?

If anyone complained at Krystina's house, he or she had to cook the next day. Paul (and lots of other people we know) had to sit at the table until he finished the food on his plate. Sheila was offered her uneaten dinner again at breakfast.

Lots of friends would find ways to secretly dispose of the food they couldn't bring themselves to eat, only to find out that their mothers always knew the dog ate their meat loaf.

This is the Clark Kent of meals—the superhero fish disguised as a burger. Mashed potato holds flaked cooked fish together, enabling you to make soft and mild-tasting "cakes," which children generally find unthreatening. You could even serve it in a hamburger bun with ketchup and call it a burger. Leave the "green bits" out of the children's fish cakes if you think it will make a difference.

1 tbsp	olive oil
1 tbsp	Dijon mustard
½ tsp	Worcestershire sauce
⅛ tsp	hot pepper sauce
1 lb	halibut or cod fillets
	Salt and freshly ground pepper
½ lb	Yukon Gold potatoes, quartered (peeled if desired)
2 tbsp	unsalted butter
1 tsp	finely chopped garlic
¼ cup	chopped green onions
2 tbsp	chopped fresh parsley
1 cup	all-purpose flour for dredging
	Vegetable oil for frying
	Lemon wedges for serving

Preheat oven to 400°F.

Combine olive oil, mustard, Worcestershire sauce and hot pepper sauce in a small bowl.

Place fish on a foil-lined baking sheet; brush with mustard mixture and season with salt and pepper to taste. Roast fish for 12 to 15 minutes or until just cooked. Let cool. Flake fish into pieces with your fingers or a fork.

While fish is cooking, place potatoes in a small pot; cover with cold water and add a pinch of salt. Bring to a boil and cook for 15 minutes or until tender. Drain water from pot and place pot with potato over low heat for about 1 minute to evaporate excess moisture. Remove from heat. Add butter and garlic; mash with a fork or potato masher. Season with salt and pepper to taste. Mixture will be quite dry. Cool.

Combine fish, mashed potato, green onions and parsley, using your hands to avoid breaking up fish too much.

Form fish mixture into 6 cakes about 3 inches in diameter and about $3/4$ inch thick. Chill until firm and ready to cook.

Heat $1/4$ inch oil in a large heavy frying pan over medium heat. Dredge fish cakes in flour; fry in batches for about 2 minutes per side or until cakes are golden and warmed through. Serve with lemon wedges.

Makes 6 fish cakes.

Weird Things Kids Like

Even the pickiest eater likes some surprising things. Here are some examples of foods that many kids like, even if they make you shudder.
• Olives
• Tzatziki
• Pickles
• Shrimp
• Sushi
• Smoked salmon
• Gummi eyeballs
• Artichokes

Chapter 9
Dessert: The Sweet Life

Have you ever noticed that kids, even babies, can identify sweets even if they have never seen anything like them in their short little lives? We've seen babies who have never had chocolate before and have yet to try anything more sophisticated than mush reach over and confidently plop a truffle into their mouths as if it were manna from heaven (and they aren't that far off). Just as babies are born with the ability to suck, they are born with knowledge of all things sugary.

Desserts can be more than mere tools for bribery. We want our kids to have a healthier attitude towards sweets than we have, don't we? To do that, we have to normalize sweets, and that means not making them forbidden food. Demonizing sugar will not make your kids healthier; it will make them sugar addicts.

We work hard to take the power out of dessert by not threatening to withhold it. As long as our kids sat at the table during dinner, they are allowed to have dessert. Before you slam this book down in disgust, we will tell you that the dessert we serve is always a child-appropriate portion, usually includes some fruit on the side and, in a lot of cases, is a nutritional part of the meal, with the added bonus of being sweet.

Oh Sugar, Sugar

Sugar's an easy scapegoat for your child's wild behaviour. But if your kids are running around screaming like wild banshees, is it because of the chocolate cake or are there other issues at play?

Sorry to burst the sucrose-induced bubble, but scientists have proven over and over again that sugar is not responsible for hyperactivity. Numerous studies have found no link between candy or chocolate and negative behaviour.

The one thing that scientists have proven is that parents expect their kids to be more energetic and aggressive after eating sugar. Think about *when* your child eats too many sweets—birthday parties, holidays. The context is more important than the food. So in short, if your kids are uncontrollable, it's all your fault (but you already knew that).

Sometimes, we don't even offer dessert, but when we do, we usually wait about 20 minutes so that whatever the kids have eaten for dinner has had some time to hit their stomachs. Occasionally, the kids will even forget about dessert. There are times, of course, when sweets are sugar- and chocolate-laden confections made for pleasure only. These are our "sometimes foods" and we love them.

We have collected some of our favourites here. Most of them are extremely simple, some of them are surprisingly nutritious, and all of them are delicious. From easy fruit desserts to trashy candy squares, these sweet treats will disappear in an instant.

Apple Crisp

We almost put this recipe in the breakfast chapter because apple crisp tastes just as delicious and is strangely appealing the morning after you make it. But no matter when you serve it, know that it is reasonably healthy and universally loved.

Be sure to use good baking apples for it—if you use the old miscellaneous apples from the back of your refrigerator (as we've been known to do) your crisp will be tasteless and watery. A good baking apple is slightly tart, and keeps its shape when cooked—rather than turning into applesauce. Northern Spy, Cortland, Ida Red, Crispin, Pink Lady and Spartan are all good baking choices.

4 lb	baking apples (about 8 large apples), peeled, cored and sliced $\frac{1}{4}$-inch thick
$\frac{1}{4}$ cup	sugar
2 tsp	grated lemon rind
2 tbsp	fresh lemon juice
1 tsp	cinnamon
$\frac{3}{4}$ cup	unsalted butter, cut into pieces
1 cup	packed brown sugar
1 cup	all-purpose flour
$\frac{3}{4}$ cup	large-flake oatmeal (not instant)
$\frac{1}{4}$ tsp	salt

Preheat oven to 375°F.

Combine apples, sugar, lemon rind, lemon juice and cinnamon in a large bowl; toss to distribute flavours. Pile apples into a 9- x 13-inch baking dish.

Combine butter, brown sugar, flour, oatmeal and salt in a medium bowl. Using your fingers or a pastry blender, work mixture until butter is the size of small peas and topping is crumbly. Sprinkle topping evenly over apples. Bake for 45 minutes or until apples are soft, juices are bubbling and topping is crisp.

Makes 6 to 8 servings.

Tip: You can use this topping to make other fresh fruit crisps.

Baked Custard

Baked custard is one of those nursery staples that has long been out of fashion, but we have good reason to bring it back—it's full of protein. The child who balks at all forms of eggs is not likely to know that the sweet treat he's eating for dessert contains more protein than the dinner that preceded it. Eshun ate these for breakfast when she was pregnant with Max because they were a quick source of protein in the morning and didn't maker her feel sick(er).

2 ½ cups	milk (preferably whole)
3	large eggs
2	large egg yolks
¼ cup	sugar
1 tbsp	vanilla
½ tsp	freshly grated nutmeg (optional)

Tip: A fancy crème brûlée sugar crust can easily be put on any custard—if you happen to have a blowtorch. Just sprinkle 1 tbsp granulated sugar on top of baked custard, light your blowtorch and, holding the flame about 2 inches away from the surface, move it in a circular motion to melt and caramelize the sugar. In theory, you can also put your sugar-topped custards under the broiler, but it just isn't the same. Plus the image of you wielding a blowtorch in the kitchen is something your kids will find impressive.

Preheat oven to 325°F.

Place 6 ¾-cup ramekins in a roasting pan.

Place milk in a medium pot and bring to a boil. Remove from heat.

Combine eggs, egg yolks, sugar and vanilla in a large bowl, whisking until mixture is uniform. Pour hot milk into egg mixture in a slow steady stream, whisking constantly so that egg mixture does not scramble. Divide custard mixture among ramekins. Sprinkle with nutmeg (if using).

Bring a kettle of water to a boil. Place a roasting pan in the oven, then carefully pour in enough boiling water to come halfway up the sides of the ramekins.

Bake custards for 28 to 30 minutes or until edges are set but centres still jiggle. Carefully remove roasting pan from oven and remove ramekins from water bath or they will keep cooking. Let cool, cover with plastic wrap and refrigerate until ready to serve.

Makes 6 custards.

Shortcakes

Why do we have two biscuit recipes in this book? They're both fast and easy to make, but this short-cake is all about being deliciously light in texture—and it's the fat that makes it so. We think berry shortcakes are a treat that deserves a comeback. Fill them with fruit and whipped cream—this is dessert, after all.

1 ½ cups	all-purpose flour
1 tbsp plus ½ tsp	sugar
2 tsp	baking powder
½ tsp	salt
1 cup	whipping cream
1 tbsp	melted butter

Tip: When it's your turn to host a baby or wedding shower, whip up 1 ½-inch shortcakes and serve them with whipped cream and strawberry preserves.

Preheat oven to 400°F.

Combine flour, 1 tbsp sugar, baking powder and salt in a medium bowl; mix well with a fork. Add whipping cream; stir with a spoon until dough just comes together.

Turn out dough onto a lightly floured surface and use your hands to flatten it to a thickness of about ³⁄₄ inch.

Use a 4-inch round cookie cutter to cut out short-cakes, gathering and flattening the scraps of dough until you have 4. Place them on a baking sheet; brush with melted butter and sprinkle with remaining sugar.

Bake for 22 minutes or until golden.

Makes 4 servings.

Baked Apples with Warm Cider Caramel

Scary Halloween Leftovers

Once your children realize the joy of collecting candy, you run the risk of being overrun with piles of teeth-decay causing, meal-spoiling treats. Here are some ideas on how to deal with it:

• Let the kids eat as much as they want that day or week, and then limit them to one treat a day.

• Let them eat as much as they want for a week, and then throw the rest out.

• Crush up all the chocolate bars and use them like chocolate chips.

• But the best idea, and one you have to start when the kids are really young is the Halloween fairy: Get your kids to set aside their favourite treats and then leave out the rest for the Halloween fairy, who comes and replaces the bags with small but desirable toys.

This is the basic baked apple all dressed up with a special sauce. Baked apples are a delicious and healthy (but don't tell the kids) dessert any day of the week, especially with a scoop of ice cream.

¼ cup	pecan halves
4	large cooking apples (Northern Spy, Pink Lady, Ida Red)
¼ cup	golden raisins, chopped
2 tbsp	light brown sugar
2 tbsp	unsalted butter, cut into small pieces
1 tbsp	grated orange rind
1 tsp	all-purpose flour
¼ tsp	cinnamon
½ cup	apple cider or juice

Cider Caramel:

½ cup	sugar
2 tbsp	orange juice

Preheat oven to 350°F.

Toast pecan halves on a baking sheet for 8 minutes or until fragrant. Remove from baking sheet and cool. Chop pecans and reserve.

Peel skin from top third of each apple. Using a melon baller or paring knife, core apples, leaving about ½ inch of the bottoms intact to hold the filling.

Combine toasted pecans, raisins, brown sugar, butter, orange rind, flour and cinnamon in a small bowl. Using a small spoon, firmly pack apples with filling. Set apples upright in a small baking dish or pie plate.

Pour apple cider over apples. Cover baking dish tightly with foil. Bake for 45 minutes or until apples can be easily pierced with a knife.

Remove apples from oven and drain apple cider juices into small pot. Cover apples to keep them warm while you make the sauce.

Heat cider and juices over medium-high heat and bring to a simmer. Simmer for 4 minutes or until juices are reduced to about $\frac{1}{4}$ cup. Remove from heat and reserve.

Cider Caramel: Heat sugar and orange juice in a small pot over medium heat, stirring until sugar has absorbed juice. Allow mixture to come to a boil; simmer for about 5 minutes or until sugar turns golden. Add reduced apple juices (stand back—the caramel will bubble and spit rather vigorously.) When bubbling subsides, stir juice and caramel until smooth and combined. Don't be tempted to stick your finger into the sauce to taste it until it has cooled slightly; molten sugar is painfully hot. Pour sauce over and around apples.

Makes 4 servings.

No Time to Bake?

Here are some other dessert ideas:
- Exotic fruit: take your kids shopping and let them pick some exotic fruit to try.
- Yogurt mixed with fruit.
- Popcorn.
- S'mores from the oven—place marshmallows on a foil-lined baking sheet and broil for 1 to 2 minutes or until puffed out and brown; sandwich each marshmallow between graham crackers with a square of chocolate.
- Grilled peach halves, pineapple wedges, bananas; sprinkle with lemon juice and brown sugar to serve.
- Chocolate dipped strawberries.
- Pretzels dipped in chocolate.
- Berries with whipped cream.
- The all-time kid favourite—Abandon the routine and go to the ice cream parlour.

Deep-dish Pear and Cranberry Pie

Deep-dish pie is really code for top crust only—which saves on both labour and calories. The kids think, and we're inclined to agree, that the pastry is the best part, but the fruit underneath is pretty delicious too. If you are pastry-phobic, buy a frozen package of puff pastry, defrost half of it and roll it out to the size of your pie plate. No one will know that you skipped a step, and your pie will still be delicious.

Radicals Hiding in the Kitchen

Parenting experts have told us that dessert can be put on the table along with dinner, and since it takes 20 minutes to feel full, if the kids eat their dessert before their broccoli, they will still have room for healthy food. We have tried it; it feels wrong, but it does it work. And it definitively takes the reward out of dessert. So once in a while, a chocolate chip cookie or frozen treat joins the main course.

Pastry:

1 ¼ cups	all-purpose flour
¼ tsp	salt
⅓ cup	cold unsalted butter, cut into pieces
¼ cup	shortening (preferably organic, trans fat–free), cut into pieces
1	large egg yolk
1–2 tbsp	cold water

Fruit Filling:

6	ripe Bartlett pears, peeled, cored and cut into thick slices (2 ½ lb)
½ cup	dried cranberries
1 tbsp	fresh lemon juice
¼ cup	sugar
2 tsp	all-purpose flour
1 tsp	cinnamon
¼ tsp	nutmeg
1 tbsp	whipping cream

Pastry: Combine flour and salt in a medium bowl. Add butter and shortening. Using your fingers or a pastry blender, work mixture until butter and shortening form clumps the size of small peas.

Beat egg yolk with 1 tbsp cold water in a small bowl. Gradually add just enough egg mixture to flour mixture to make dough hold together. Add another tbsp or so of cold water if mixture is too dry. Wrap dough in plastic wrap and chill for 30 minutes.

Preheat oven to 400°F.

Fruit Filling: Combine pears, dried cranberries, lemon juice, sugar, flour, cinnamon and nutmeg in a large bowl; toss to distribute flavours. Pile fruit mixture into a 9-inch pie plate.

Place pastry on a lightly floured surface and roll out to fit pie plate. Lay pastry over fruit and trim to within $1/2$ inch of the pie plate rim. Tuck edge of pastry into pie plate, enclosing fruit. Brush pastry with whipping cream. Cut a few slits in pastry to let steam escape.

Bake for 50 minutes or until fruit is bubbling and pastry is golden.

Makes 4 to 6 servings.

Let Them Eat Cake

"Owen doesn't eat pizza, which is annoying, but only becomes a crisis at birthday parties. At first we wouldn't let him eat the birthday cake unless he had one bite of pizza. But then we realized that a party with his friends is not a place for discipline. Now we just let him eat cake, and on days when we have two birthday parties, he just eats nutritionally absent cake twice in a day. We just hope for a spare minute to cram something healthy into him."
Cathy

One-pot Brownies

If you like light and cakey brownies, look elsewhere. These are dark, rich and fudgey. They will cure the blues on any day and leave everyone begging for more. You can make 32 small brownies or 12 huge ones. Warning: no matter what size they are, you will go back for seconds, maybe even thirds.

For a nut-free version, substitute finely chopped dried cherries, desiccated coconut, very adult crystallized ginger or something like Skor bits (but nothing that melts, or the brownies will not set). Can you just skip the additions? Yes, but then your brownies would be considerably smaller and that would not be a good thing.

½ cup	unsalted butter, cut into pieces
2 oz	bittersweet chocolate, chopped
1 cup	sugar
2	large eggs, beaten
½ cup	all-purpose flour
¼ cup	cocoa powder, sifted (preferably Dutch-process)
½ tsp	salt
½ tsp	vanilla
½ cup	chopped pecans or walnuts
½ cup	chocolate chips

Preheat oven to 350° F.

Grease an 8-inch square baking pan and line the bottom and 2 sides of the pan with parchment paper or foil.

Melt butter and chocolate in a heavy pot over low heat. Remove from heat; stir in sugar and eggs until combined. Add flour, cocoa powder and salt; stir until just incorporated. Add vanilla, nuts and chocolate chips; stir to distribute evenly.

Spread batter in prepared pan. Bake for 25 minutes or until brownies are set and a cake tester comes out with crumbs clinging to it. Do not overbake.

Allow brownies to cool in pan on a wire rack (or in the refrigerator if you're in a hurry). Transfer brownies from pan to a cutting board. Using a sharp knife, cut into whatever size desired.

Makes up to 32 brownies.

Real Fruit Gelatin

It wiggles, it wobbles, and it's your own personal science experiment. Homemade gelatin desserts are more nutritious (or at least less bad for you) than the mix. Try different fruit juice combinations to find fun and delicious flavours (but avoid pineapple and kiwi, as the enzymes in the fruit keep the gelatin from setting). Once you've got the technique down, start adding chunks of fruit, just like Mom used to.

1 cup	water
2	packages unflavoured gelatin (or 2 tbsp)
3 cups	fruit juice

Pour water into a small pot and sprinkle with gelatin. Let stand for 1 minute. Warm over low heat, stirring, until gelatin is dissolved. Remove from heat.

Pour gelatin mixture into a large bowl. Whisking to combine, slowly add juice to gelatin mixture. Transfer to a bowl or an 8-inch square pan; refrigerate until set (about 1 hour). Cut into cubes or spoon into bowls to serve.

Makes 4 servings.

Grapes of Wrath

We have a weird thing about those little stems on grapes. So as soon as we bring the grapes home, we wash them and cut them in lovely kid-sized bunches, discarding the huge "leader" stem, and place them in a big bowl in the fridge. We are then safe in the knowledge that the ugly branches will be thrown out immediately and we won't have a bunch of widowed stems peppered with only a few grapes sitting in the fridge.

Real Vanilla Pudding

Good News for All

Studies have shown that the antioxidant levels in 2 tbsp of cocoa power are higher than those in red wine and green or black tea. Say goodbye to Alzheimer's while you and the kids enjoy some hot cocoa or brownies—or both!

Once you taste homemade pudding, Bill Cosby will be out of your life forever. Unlike the packaged kind, homemade pudding is full of protein and calcium. Adults, kids and babies will love it plain or fancied up with warmed seasonal fruit or chocolate sauce. If there are any leftovers, they make great, drip-free frozen pops.

2 ½ cups	whole milk
¼ cup	cornstarch
½ cup	sugar
1	large egg
2	large egg yolks
2 tbsp	unsalted butter, cut into small pieces
1 tbsp	vanilla

Tip: How about a delicious, warm fruit topping to go with your pudding? Combine 1 ½ cups blueberries, 1 ½ cups peeled, sliced peaches and 1 tbsp sugar; let sit for 15 minutes or until fruit juices are released. Place pot over medium heat and cook, stirring occasionally, for 5 minutes or until fruit is warmed through and bursting with juice. Serve warm or at room temperature as a topping for the pudding.

Place 2 cups of the milk in a medium heavy-bottomed pot and bring to a boil. Remove from heat.

Meanwhile, sift cornstarch and sugar together into a medium bowl. Add remaining $1/2$ cup milk, egg and egg yolks; whisk to combine.

Pour hot milk into egg mixture in a slow steady stream, whisking constantly so that mixture becomes uniform without scrambling eggs. Return mixture to pot; cook over medium heat, whisking constantly, until mixture comes to a boil and is thick enough to coat wires of whisk, about 4 to 5 minutes. Remove from heat. Add butter and vanilla, stirring until mixture is uniform.

Pour pudding through a strainer into a clean bowl or ramekins; press plastic wrap right onto surface of pudding to prevent a "skin" from forming. Chill until ready to serve.

Makes 4 servings.

Variation: Chocolate Pudding
Using the same method as Real Vanilla Pudding, sift 3 tbsp Dutch-process cocoa along with the cornstarch and sugar. Decrease the amount of sugar to $1/3$ cup. Decrease vanilla to 1 tsp. Stir in 4 oz melted chopped bittersweet chocolate along with the vanilla.

Tip: We firmly believe that great flavour comes from using high-quality ingredients. When we say vanilla, we mean pure vanilla extract, which is expensive but has a flavour unmatched by imitation extracts. The chocolate you use to make your cookies, brownies or puddings should be delicious enough to eat on its own. Look for big bars of Callebaut, Valrhona or Lindt bittersweet chocolate, and chop them up to use in your baked goods. Yes, they're more expensive than baking chocolate, but you and your family are worth it—and on a night when you don't feel like baking, you and your kids can enjoy it as is!

Rice Pudding

Yes, you can use that container of steamed white rice left over from last night's take-out dinner and skip the first two steps, though rice pudding does taste a bit better with freshly cooked rice. We like the flavour and texture of basmati rice in our pudding, but use whichever kind your family prefers.

1 cup	basmati or other rice (or 4 cups cooked rice)
4 cups	whole milk
½ cup	sugar
½ cup	raisins (optional)
1	egg
½ cup	cream or whole milk
½ tsp	vanilla
⅛ tsp	cinnamon

Eggstremely Good

We have been scared into thinking that raw eggs are dangerous. Experts say about one in 10,000 eggs is contaminated with salmonella bacteria and that you should use caution when cooking for young children, the elderly, pregnant women and anyone with a compromised immune system. That being said, childhood would not be the same without eating raw cookie dough, and if our kids are willing to eat the delicious runny yolk of a soft-boiled egg, we're all for it.

Rinse rice in cold water until water runs clear; drain.

Add rice to a pot along with 1 ½ cups water and bring to a boil. Cover, turn down heat to low and cook for 15 minutes or until water is absorbed and rice is almost fully cooked. Remove from heat and allow rice to steam, covered, for 5 minutes.

Place cooked rice in a large pot along with milk, sugar and raisins. Bring to a boil (watching that it doesn't boil over). Turn down heat to medium-low and simmer, uncovered, for 20 minutes or until rice is very tender and most of the milk has been absorbed.

Beat egg, cream and vanilla in a medium bowl. Stir in about 1 cup of the hot rice mixture (to keep the egg mixture from scrambling). Stir remaining egg mixture into rice mixture until fully combined. The hot milk and rice mixture will cook egg thoroughly. (If you are really concerned about the eggs being cooked, continue to stir it over low heat for 2 minutes. Use a candy or instant-read thermometer—eggs are fully cooked at 160°F.)

Sprinkle cinnamon into pudding. Transfer pudding to a serving bowl or individual ramekins. Serve warm or chilled.

Makes 4 to 6 servings.

Frozen Banana Treats

This is a banana split on the go. Let your imagination and your children's tastes guide you—these can be very healthy or a real treat depending on what you coat the bananas with.

4	small bananas, peeled
1 cup	vanilla yogurt
	OR
4 oz	melted white or dark chocolate
2 cups	finely chopped pecans,
	finely chopped dried cranberries,
	desiccated coconut, mini M&M's,
	candy sprinkles, etc.
4	flat wooden craft sticks

Line a baking sheet with parchment or waxed paper. Push wooden sticks into one end of each banana.

Pour yogurt or melted chocolate into a shallow bowl. Pour desired topping ingredients into another shallow bowl.

Working with one at a time, lay bananas in yogurt or chocolate, turning to coat well, then roll in toppings, patting so that they stick well.

Lay bananas on prepared baking sheet; place in the freezer until coatings have hardened. Transfer to a sealed plastic bag until ready to eat.

Makes 4 servings.

Which Are You?

If you have two children, you will notice that one is a hoarder of treats and the other is a binger. Usually the oldest child has stashes of candy hidden throughout the house getting stale, but child number two has gobbled it all up in seconds flat, for fear that someone else will get to it.

Orange Melon Frozen Pops

Homemade ice pops are a dessert staple. And sometimes even a breakfast treat. This mixture combines tangy orange taste with the nutritional benefits of cantaloupe and mango.

2 cups	diced ripe cantaloupe
1 cup	mango juice
½ cup	unsweetened frozen orange juice concentrate

Place cantaloupe, mango juice and orange juice concentrate in a blender or food processor; process until smooth. Pour mixture through a strainer to remove any stray chunks. Pour into ice pop moulds and freeze overnight or until frozen solid.

When ready to serve, run warm water over the outside of mould to help release ice pops.

Makes 3 cups ice pop mixture. The number of ice pops will vary depending on the size of your moulds.

Wishy-Washy

Some parents wouldn't dream of giving their kids an unwashed piece of fruit. We, however, will offer them whatever we can without delay, and if that means unwashed grapes in the grocery store, so be it. The FDA does recommend washing fruits and vegetables before eating because soil, dirt and bacteria (i.e., yicky communicable diseases) can linger on the fruit's skin. Washing under a steady stream of water and a light scrub with a brush will definitely do the job. We take the sticker off as we wash the fruit—if the sticker is still on it, we know it needs a quick wash. Just so you know, washing fruit with only water will not remove any pesticides; give it a thorough scrub with a bit of soap. And the fruit and veggie wash in a bottle is not any better than soap.

Chocolate
Candy Squares

No two ways about it—this is strictly a treat. So if you want to spoil your kids, wow them on their birthdays or sell out at the bake sale table, this is the one.

We Won't Tell

Sometimes one chocolate is not enough. One potato chip doesn't do it, and even two don't satisfy. It's okay and even healthy for you and your kids to totally over-indulge once in a while—guilt-free. So surprise yourself and your kids—say yes to their outrageous requests—sometimes.

8 oz	bittersweet chocolate, finely chopped
2 oz	white chocolate, finely chopped
¾ cup	whipping cream
¼ cup	unsalted butter, softened and cut into small cubes
1 cup	graham cracker crumbs
¼ cup	finely shredded unsweetened coconut
½ cup	mini or regular M&M's, or similar candy

Line an 8-inch square baking pan with plastic wrap.

Place bittersweet chocolate and white chocolate in separate bowls.

Pour whipping cream into a small pot and bring to a boil. Remove from heat.

Pour $\frac{1}{2}$ cup whipping cream over dark chocolate and remaining $\frac{1}{4}$ cup over white chocolate. Stir in cream until chocolates are melted. Add butter to dark chocolate mixture; stir until butter is melted and mixture is uniform and glossy.

Stir graham cracker crumbs into dark chocolate mixture; pour into prepared pan, spreading it out to corners.

Stir coconut into white chocolate mixture; pour over dark chocolate mixture. If desired, use the tip of a knife to swirl dark chocolate through white chocolate.

If using regular-size M&M's, place in a sealed plastic bag and crush into small pieces with a rolling pin or mallet.

Sprinkle mini or crushed M&M's over white chocolate; place pan in the refrigerator to chill for 2 hours or until set.

To serve, pull on a corner of the plastic wrap and the solid chocolate bar will come out of the pan. Place on a cutting board and cut into 64 small squares. Serve chilled or at room temperature.

Makes 64 squares.

Beware the Bake Sale

Bake sales are a strangely competitive place, and if you want to be the one to sell out first, here's what you need to remember: sprinkles, Smarties and M&M's. It doesn't matter what you make (it could even be a mix, horrors!), as long as you top it with copious amounts of brightly coloured candy.

PARTY!

Chapter 10
Parties: They Ain't What They Used to Be

Once in a while, you will have to emerge from your cave and have people over. Whether it's for birthday parties, mothers' groups or even, gasp, an adult-only meal, you may find that you even enjoy throwing a party.

To start off, you must have a first birthday party, as much for you as for your little one. A first birthday is a bittersweet celebration that you throw for yourself and family—a celebration of making it through that terrifying first year. But as your kids get older, the birthday parties morph into beasts that belch out loot bags full of crappy toys and cakes made in the shapes of their favourite TV characters. Emma's mother always said that birthday parties were the most stressful days of the year, and she may be right. Your children are depending on you to satisfy every one of their outlandish desires and remain calm while doing it.

As for REAL entertaining, you may be shaking your head at the mere thought of having adults over to your child-ruled home. But you *can* do it! Planning is key to even the most casual of get-togethers; the shopping, preparation and actual event may be spread over many days, leaving you plenty of time to tidy up the kids' messes before anyone arrives. Your child-less guests—if you still socialize with them at all—won't have any idea how much more work it is to have them over for dinner now (although the fact that it's taken you a year to reciprocate their dinner invitation might give them a clue), and the friends who do have kids will be so amazed at what you pulled off, they wouldn't dream of being critical about the unvacuumed floor and piles of toys stuffed into baskets in the corners.

Despite the stress, it is very confidence building to actually throw a successful party, proving that you can multi-task on the grandest of scales. And you have a choice: to either make it look as if you pulled out all the stops or as if you haven't lifted a finger. We have menus for both.

Some of these menus include recipes pulled from other chapters in the book, and we've added some recipes here that we wouldn't expect you to make unless people were coming over. We are big fans of mixing store-bought items with homemade. So buy a rotisserie chicken to toss in your pasta. Buy some hors d'oeuvres, a pre-made sauce and a pack-aged salad. Mix and match these recipes with some of your own favourites from the pre-kid years, but most importantly, don't be afraid to invite people over. It is possible to have an adult conversation in your home and eat something other than pizza, and it's really important to remember what that feels like.

Pay for It!

When it comes to parties, the best, most useful advice comes from our friend Judy: "Hire someone!" Whether it's a teenager from down the street to help keep the kids entertained and get them ready for bed, or someone to do cleanup in the kitchen—having an extra pair of hands around is well worth the money (and very addictive)!

Kid-Free
Dinner Party

Having an adults-only dinner never ceases to be a big deal—it's like you are playing at being grown-ups. So enjoy it! Start by buying the nibbles, and if people offer to bring something, say yes. It's better than getting more soap as a hostess gift. And don't forget to pour yourself a glass of wine about 30 minutes before the guests arrive.

- Purchased appetizers
- Indulgent Mashed Potatoes (page 109)
- Osso Buco (page 186–187)
- Green Beans with Pecans and Brown Butter (page 110)
- Deep-dish Pear and Cranberry Pie (page 170)

- Purchased dips, a wedge of Parmesan, and some prosciutto.
- Bowls of nuts, wasabi peas, or olives.
- Cheese fondue can be found at most supermarkets; microwave it and serve with baguette slices and crudités.
- Chop up some sun-dried tomatoes and herbs and roll a piece of goat cheese through it; drizzle with olive oil and serve with crackers.
- Slice a baguette into thin rounds, brush with olive oil and toast in the oven until crisp. Top with something from the Italian market: marinated artichokes, tapenade, Italian canned tuna mixed with capers and herbs, chopped tomatoes and pesto.
- Pick up some spring rolls at the local Asian restaurant, or samosas from your favourite Indian restaurant.

Osso Buco

This is a perfect company-coming-over dish because you can prepare it the day before. In fact, it tastes better if done a day ahead. So whip it up during nap time (if your child doesn't nap, that's a whole other set of problems).

Veal shanks are available at most butcher shops. Ask the butcher to cut them for you so they are the same size. And because it's a braise, the oven times are approximate, so if you forget about it and leave it in there a bit longer, it won't matter too much. Even kids like this—just tell them it's ribs.

2 tsp	chopped fresh rosemary
2 tsp	chopped fresh thyme
1 tsp	freshly ground pepper
$\frac{1}{2}$ tsp	ground coriander
4	large veal shanks, cut 1½-inch thick (4–5 lb)
	Salt
3 tbsp	olive oil
2 oz	bacon or pancetta, chopped
1 cup	chopped onion
1 cup	chopped carrots
$\frac{1}{2}$ cup	chopped celery
2 tbsp	chopped garlic
3	3- x ½-inch strips lemon peel
2	small bay leaves
2 tsp	chopped fresh thyme
2 cups	white wine or dry vermouth
2 cups	canned tomatoes, squished up and drained
1 ½ cups	chicken or veal stock (homemade or low-sodium)
	Salt and freshly ground pepper

Gremolata:

3 tbsp	chopped fresh parsley
1 tbsp	grated lemon rind
1 tsp	chopped garlic
$\frac{1}{2}$ tsp	freshly ground pepper

Preheat oven to 350°F.

Combine rosemary, thyme, pepper and coriander in small bowl. Rub all over veal shanks; season with salt to taste.

Heat oil in a Dutch oven or large ovenproof pot over medium-high heat. Add veal shanks; sear for 4 minutes per side or until well browned. Transfer to a plate and reserve.

Reduce heat to medium. Add bacon to pot; sauté for 1 minute. Add onions, carrots and celery; cover pot and cook, stirring occasionally, for 10 minutes, or until vegetables are soft. Add garlic, lemon peel, bay leaves and thyme. Pour in wine and bring to a boil, scraping up brown bits. Add tomatoes and stock. Return veal to pot; bring to boil. Cover and transfer pot to oven. Cook, covered and turning occasionally for about 1 ½ hours or until tender.

Gremolata: Combine parsley, lemon rind, garlic and pepper in small bowl.

Remove pot from oven. Remove meat and skim off any fat that rises to top. Place pot over medium heat; boil, uncovered, until sauce reduces enough to coat spoon. Season with salt and pepper to taste. Discard lemon peel and bay leaves. Serve veal with sauce and sprinkle with gremolata.

Makes 4 servings.

Party Prep for Pooped Parents

Cleaning up is a state of mind, as in "out of sight, out of mind," so don't worry about throwing things in closets, under beds and in the kids' rooms. Only clean the one bathroom and the two rooms your guests will use.

Mothers' Groups

These women may turn out to be your lifelong friends, even if the only thing you initially have in common is that your children wear the same size diaper. So how do you impress them but not look so good that you can't complain about your life? Offer up an easy menu that can be eaten with one hand and includes lots of chocolate and maybe a bottle (or two) of wine.

- Giant Panini
- Salad Niçoise
- One-pot Brownies (page 172)
- For the kids: bowls of small crackers, a fruit plate (comprised of fruits that don't stain), mini yogurts (kept in a bowl of ice), mini-muffins or cut-up cheese or jam sandwiches

Giant Panini Sandwich

Paninis are taking over the world, and let's be honest—some of them are not so good. But not the ones you make at home. You don't need to order a panini maker from the Shopping Channel. You can mimic the expensive restaurant presses by using a grill pan or frying pan as the base and then another frying pan weighed down by several heavy cans of beans or vegetables as the "lid" to compress your sandwich. Use pieces of thin focaccia or another flatbread that will fit your pan; slice and fill with your favourite toppings. Cook over medium heat with the "lid" pressing down and flip after 3 minutes or whenever the bread is golden. You can assemble the sandwiches well ahead of time and then cook them when the company arrives, or even reheat cooked sandwiches in a 350°F oven for 8 minutes or until warmed through.

Experiment with combos such as smoked turkey, havarti and baby arugula, prosciutto and goat cheese, ham and Gruyère, tuna salad and Cheddar. Just don't choose fillings that are too wet, and don't use too much filling or the sandwich won't hold together.

Salade Niçoise

Salad Niçoise made with fresh tuna is such a special treat. It's bound to make you and your guests feel spoiled, and since it doesn't wilt, it's great as part of a buffet lunch. Traditionally, this salad should include hard-boiled eggs but we're split on the issue, so decide for yourself. If you can't find fresh tuna, or don't want to spend the money, you can substitute three cans of solid white tuna, drained and broken into pieces, or try the indulgent Italian tuna packed in olive oil.

Dressing:

⅓ cup	olive oil
2 tbsp	red wine vinegar
1 tbsp	balsamic vinegar
½ tsp	liquid honey
1 tbsp	finely chopped shallots
	Salt and freshly ground pepper

Salad:

1 tbsp	olive oil
12 oz	fresh tuna, cut about ½-inch thick
1 lb	mini red-skinned potatoes, cut in half
8 oz	thin green beans, stem end removed and halved if long
1 ½ cups	cherry tomatoes, halved
½ cup	black olives, preferably Niçoise or Kalamata

Dressing: Combine olive oil, red wine vinegar, balsamic vinegar, honey and shallots in a small bowl; whisk to combine. Season with salt and pepper to taste.

Salad: Season tuna with salt and pepper. Heat olive oil in a frying pan over medium-high heat. Add tuna and sear for 1 to 2 minutes per side or until tuna is browned on the outside but still slightly rare in the centre. Cool. Cut into ½-inch cubes.

Place potatoes in a medium pot with enough cold salted water to cover; bring to a boil. Boil for 8 minutes or until tender. Drain. Toss with half of the dressing. Set aside.

Bring a small pot of salted water to a boil; add green beans and blanch for 3 minutes or until tender-crisp. Drain, then dunk in ice water to stop the cooking. Set aside.

Combine potatoes and green beans with cherry tomatoes and olives in a large bowl.

Add dressing and toss to coat. Add seared tuna and toss gently to combine. Taste and adjust seasonings if necessary.

Makes 6 to 8 servings.

Dinner for Two

Once you have kids, the relationship between you and your spouse can seem like a far-off memory. But spending time as a couple is good for both of you *and* good for the kids. Even if you have to eat at 10 p.m., it's worth the effort to have dinner *à deux* once in a while. And we know you can find something to talk about other than the kids. This lamb rack is easy to make, and chocolate fondue a dreamy pleasure for you both.

- Rack of Lamb
- Roasted Root Vegetables (page 115)
- Quick Dark Greens Sauté (page 111)
- Chocolate Fondue

Rack of Lamb

Rack of lamb is not scary to prepare; it's actually quite easy and is both refined and sexy. Just like you.

2	racks of lamb (1¼ lb)
¾ cup	chopped fresh mint
2 tbsp	olive oil
2 tsp	Worcestershire sauce
1 tsp	chopped garlic
	Salt and freshly ground pepper
¼ cup	red wine
1 cup	chicken stock (homemade or low-sodium)
2 tsp	tomato paste

Preheat oven to 400°F.

Use a sharp knife to score fat on the back of the lamb racks in an X pattern. Heat an ovenproof frying pan over medium heat. Add the rack, fat side down; cook for 2 minutes per side or until meat is browned. Remove from heat.

Combine ½ cup mint, olive oil, Worcestershire sauce and garlic in a small bowl.

Remove lamb from frying pan; rub with mint mixture and season with salt and pepper to taste. Return to pan fat side up and place in oven; roast for 20 minutes or until cooked to desired degree of doneness.

Remove lamb from frying pan and allow to rest in a warm place while you make the sauce. Be careful: handle will be searing hot.

Discard fat from frying pan. Place on stove over medium heat. Pour in red wine and reduce to 1 tbsp. Add chicken stock and bring to a boil; boil for 8 minutes or until thickened slightly. Whisk in tomato paste. Add remaining ¼ cup fresh mint. Season with salt and pepper to taste. Serve lamb racks sliced into chops with a puddle of sauce for dipping.

Makes 2 servings.

Chocolate Fondue

This has got to be the simplest, most decadent dessert. And the recipe is easily doubled if you have a family of chocoholics. Keep fondue warm and liquid by putting it in a stand over a tea light or on the lowest setting of a hot plate, but don't use a traditional fondue pot as it will get too hot and the chocolate will burn. Serve with berries, chunks of fresh fruit, dried fruit, cubes of cake, cookies or even marshmallows.

Pour 1/4 cup whipping cream into a small pot and bring to a boil. Remove from heat and add 4 oz chopped bittersweet chocolate (about 3/4 cup); stir until chocolate is melted and mixture is smooth. Keep in a warm spot or gently reheat when ready to serve. Transfer to a small serving bowl placed over very low heat. Surround with fruit and other accompaniments. Makes 2 to 4 servings.

Invite the
Neighbours Over

Sometimes it's just too much to inflict our kids on any of our childless friends, so we find that the most common form of entertaining we do is to have other crazy families over. It can be kind of hectic, and sometimes the kids don't eat too much, but it's fun and a great way to kill that period between late afternoon and bedtime.

- Lucy Waverman's Up-North Flank Steak
- Simplest Caesar Salad (page 107)
- Garlic-Roasted Carrots (page 109)
- Spiced Oven Home Fries (page 112)
- Apple Crisp (page 165)

Lucy Waverman's
Up-North
Flank Steak

Imagine growing up in a house where every meal was delicious but was often a strange mélange of dishes—salsas to start, Indian curries for the main course and some nouvelle Canadian cuisine invention for a side dish. That was Emma's experience growing up with a famous food writer and teacher as a mother. This made Emma picky in a very peculiar way: as a child she rejected macaroni and cheese, canned tomato sauce made her shudder, and she was not a very popular lunch guest at her friends' houses. Lucy Waverman has inspired many great cooks and great eaters, and she is also Eshun's long-standing employer. This is one of her most popular recipes.

1 1/2 lb	flank steak
3 tbsp	balsamic vinegar
3 tbsp	olive oil
1 tbsp	Dijon mustard
1 tbsp	chopped garlic

Horseradish Mustard Butter:

4 oz	unsalted butter, softened
1 tbsp	Dijon mustard
1 tbsp	grated horseradish

Use a sharp knife to score one side of the flank steak in a cross-hatch pattern. Whisk together vinegar, oil, mustard and garlic; pour over steak. Marinate for 2 hours or overnight in the refrigerator.

Horseradish Mustard Butter: Beat together butter, mustard and horseradish. Form into a log and roll in a sheet of waxed paper. Refrigerate.

Preheat the broiler or grill to high. Broil steak for about 4 minutes on one side and 3 minutes on the other for rare. Let rest on carving board for 5 minutes.

Slice steak against the grain into thin slices. Slice Horseradish Mustard Butter into thin slices and serve with steak.

Makes 4 servings.

First Birthday Party

The first birthday is bittersweet: you are happy that your little one is growing up but you're sad to say goodbye to Baby. You made it through the first year and that deserves a celebration. Brunch is definitely the easiest (you have to get up early anyway). And after the party, you can all collapse into a big family nap—which you'll need after staying up into the wee hours to ice the cake.

- Grilled vegetable platter: buy pre-grilled veggies or thinly slice zucchini and eggplant; toss in olive oil, sprinkle with salt and pepper and grill until just cooked through, along with portobello mushroom caps, halved red, yellow, and green peppers, and thick spears of asparagus.
- Bagels with deli-style cream cheese and smoked salmon
- Egg Salad (page 73)
- Tuna Salad (page 72)
- Beyond Boxed Macaroni and Cheese (page 94)
- Vanilla Birthday Cake with Homestyle Butter Icing

Vanilla
Birthday Cake

All cooks need a plain white cake in their reper-toire, and this is it. It can be used for all occasions: birthdays, tea parties, surprise guests coming over. Pretty it up with Homestyle Butter Icing (page 197) or Chocolate Icing (page 201).

2 cups	all-purpose flour
1 tsp	baking powder
1/4 tsp	salt
1/2 cup	unsalted butter, softened
1 1/2 cups	sugar
2	large eggs
1 tsp	vanilla
1 cup	buttermilk

Preheat oven to 325°F.

Tip: You can vary the flavour of this cake by adding 1 tbsp grated lemon or orange rind, or 1 cup finely chopped nuts, chocolate, thinly sliced apples, peaches or even blueberries to the batter. Try filling the cooled cake layers with icing, lemon curd, jam, dulce de leche or whatever suits the occasion and your child's tastes.

Grease 2 9-inch round cake pans and line the bot-toms with parchment paper.

Combine flour, baking powder and salt in a small bowl; stir with a fork to blend.

Beat together butter and sugar with an electric mixer until light and fluffy. Add eggs, one at a time, beating well between additions. Add vanilla extract and beat until incorporated.

Add a third of the flour mixture to the batter, beating until combined. Add half of the buttermilk. Repeat, alternating ingredients, until all flour mixture and buttermilk have been incorporated.

Divide batter between prepared pans. Bake for 50 to 60 minutes or until cakes are golden brown and a cake tester comes out clean. Cool cakes in pans for 10 minutes. Running a knife around the edge of the pans to loosen cakes, turn out onto a rack. Peel parchment paper from bottoms of cakes and allow to cool completely. Fill and frost.

Makes 12 servings.

Decorating the $#@! Cake

Unfortunately, we have become slaves to our children's whims when it comes to their birthday cakes. We want the little ones to be happy, but not at the cost of our last shred of sanity. We urge you to keep it simple, as simple can often look better than ridiculously complicated. We will rent pans and do cakes in silly shapes. We will do a Barbie skirt cake, and we will make a castle. We will not make a three-dimensional train, and we will not do anything that entails lots of writing with icing. But we will stay up until 1 a.m. to ice the cake. It's sort of a family tradition. Here are some tricks we have picked up over the years.

For those who have never baked and iced a birthday cake, or only make one or two a year, a word to the wise: it will look homemade. But that's sort of the point. Otherwise, you can buy an airbrushed creation from the grocery store that will taste just as pre-fab as it looks. Kids love coloured icing, and they're often very happy with a round cake that has some small recognizable toys on the top among the birthday candles (think blue icing topped with little rubber ducks). And when in doubt, lots of sprinkles, Smarties and jellybeans make all kids (even the grown ones) happy.

Some supermarkets and bulk stores rent out cake pans in the shapes of dinosaurs or fire trucks or cartoon characters, which take a while to ice but are straightforward and definitely a big hit. Or you could buy a star-shaped pan and make that your standard cake, decorating it differently each time.

Baking a cake in a stainless steel bowl gives you lots of options, but beware—it takes a while to get the centre baked. You can make the ubiquitous Barbie cake by shoving the doll into the middle of the round cake and decorating her skirt with coloured icing and candies. Ladybugs, soccer balls and base-balls can also be made out of baked-in-a-bowl cakes.

Two layers of round cakes can be put side by side to make a figure eight. Add cookie crumbs for roads and dirt piles, dyed green coconut "grass," and toy cars and trains "driving" on top (see opposite).

Cupcakes with each guest's initials piped on top are a big hit with everyone!

Homestyle Butter Icing

There are some things to know about icing. If you want really stiff icing for piping and decorating, you may need to add more sugar or, gasp, some short-ening. For really vibrant colours, use the paste icing found at specialty stores. And if you need to make red icing for certain Sesame Street characters, then you need to use all shortening because butter plus red food colouring makes it pink, no matter how much concentrated red you use.

1 cup	unsalted butter (2 sticks), softened
1 tsp	vanilla
5 cups	icing sugar
1–2 tbsp	milk

Cream butter with an electric mixer. Add vanilla and blend. Gradually add sugar, 1 cup at a time, beating well on medium speed. Scrape sides and bottom of bowl often. (Icing may appear to be dry.) Add 1 tbsp milk; beat at medium speed until light and fluffy, adding more milk if icing seems dry.

Keep icing in the refrigerator until ready to use. Store in an airtight container for up to 2 weeks. You may need to rewhip before using.

Makes 3 cups, enough to frost a 9-inch 2-layer cake.

Third Birthday Party and Beyond

Third and fourth birthday parties are complicated—your kids have their own friends they want invited and most parents will stay and nibble, so make sure there is some adult-friendly food around too. And yes, bowls of chips with store-bought dip is fine.

By the time your kid turns five, it's a kid free-for-all, and you will find yourself alone with ten of them. You may have to provide some kind of hired entertainment or your house will be in total shambles. If you have an amazingly creative adult in your life who can make up a treasure hunt and run some simple party games, utilize those skills fully. If you don't know anybody who could pull this off, wear earplugs, keep your sense of humour and make sure everyone leaves at the designated time!

- Make your own pizzas (see page 101 for the dough recipe): Make the dough ahead of time and have the toppings laid out (make sure you have lots of cheese!). After the kids have made their masterpieces, write their names on a piece of parchment that will go under the pizzas while they are baking.
- Festive Fruit Kabobs
- Chocolate Birthday Cake or Cupcakes with Chocolate Icing (see over)

Festive Fruit Kabobs

So Martha with so little effort. Use small cookie cutters to cut stars, squares and circles out of slices of melon, papaya and so forth, then stick them on wooden skewers interspersed with whole strawberries and slices of kiwi. Top off with blueberries and raspberries. Watermelon is the best for colour and size, and even makes lots of skewers on its own. Keep the fruit trimmings in the freezer for smoothies.

Setting the Scene

Get kids involved in their parties by reviving the old-fashioned use of name cards at the table. It could take them at least an hour to write all the names on the cards and decorate them, just long enough for you to get something done.

Chocolate Birthday Cake

The classic simple chocolate cake—think how good you'll look in front of the other parents when you tell them that you did not use a mix. This cake is delicious enough for the adults and yummy the next day straight out of the fridge.

4 oz	bittersweet chocolate, chopped into small pieces (about ³/₄ cup)
2 ¼ cups	all-purpose flour
½ cup	cocoa powder (not Dutch-process)
1 ½ tsp	baking soda
1 tsp	salt
1 cup	unsalted butter, softened
1 ½ cups	sugar
3	large eggs
1 tsp	vanilla
2 cups	buttermilk

Tip: This recipe also makes 30 cupcakes—bake them for 20 minutes.

Preheat oven to 350°F.

Grease 2 9-inch round cake pans and line bottoms with parchment paper.

Place chocolate in a small, heavy-bottomed pot over low heat; stir until almost melted. Remove from heat and stir until fully melted. Cool to room temperature.

Sift together flour, cocoa powder, baking soda and salt into a medium bowl.

Beat together butter and sugar with an electric mixer until light and fluffy. Add eggs, one at a time, beating well between additions. Add vanilla and melted chocolate; beat until uniform. Add a third of the flour mixture to the batter, beating until combined. Add half of the buttermilk. Repeat until all flour mixture and buttermilk have been incorporated.

Divide batter between prepared pans. Bake for 45 minutes or until a cake tester comes out clean. Cool cakes in pans for 10 minutes. Running a knife around the edge of the pans to loosen cakes, turn out onto a rack. Peel parchment paper from bottoms of cakes and allow to cool completely. Fill and frost.

Makes 12 servings.

Chocolate Icing

A simply delicious chocolate icing that is sweet enough for the kids without giving the adults a toothache. But please keep in mind that the better the chocolate, the better the icing.

¹⁄₂ cup	milk
¹⁄₃ cup	unsalted butter, cut into pieces
6 oz	chopped bittersweet chocolate (about 1 cup)
1 ¹⁄₂ cups	icing sugar, sifted
¹⁄₄ cup	cocoa powder (preferably Dutch-process)

Combine milk and butter in a medium pot; bring to a boil. Remove from heat. Add chocolate; stir until chocolate is melted and mixture is smooth.

Sift together icing sugar and cocoa powder. Add sugar and cocoa mixture to chocolate mixture a bit at a time; stir until smooth.

Allow icing to cool in the refrigerator or at room temperature until it is spreadable.

Makes enough icing to fill and frost a 9-inch 2-layer cake.

Tip: When we call for cocoa powder we mean unsweetened. Cocoa powder comes in two types: "Dutch-process," which is what Fry's, Droste and some supermarket brands are, and "regular" or "American," the most easily found being Hershey's and Ghirardelli. These two types of cocoa powder aren't interchangeable: the regular is richer and more bitter than Dutch-process, and they have different chemical breakdowns. Regular cocoa powder is a little harder to find in Canada (look for it in upscale grocery stores and gourmet shops) but it is what makes our cake so deliciously dark and fudgy. Dutch-process cocoa powder is ideal almost anywhere else.

Chapter 11
Picky Pantry

This is the essential non-perishables list. If you were just starting out, you could take this list with you to the grocery store and spend hundreds of dollars just like that. So, of course, we're not saying you have to buy all these things right now, but if you start stocking your cupboards and refrigerator with these ingredients, you will have the basis for all the recipes in this book and a whole lot more besides. Happy cooking!

Oils, Vinegars and Condiments for the Cupboard

Olive oil (preferably extra-virgin)
Vegetable oil (canola and safflower are the healthiest)
Sesame oil
Red wine vinegar
White wine vinegar
Balsamic vinegar
Cider vinegar
Rice wine vinegar (seasoned)
Hot pepper sauce (Tabasco, etc.)
Worcestershire sauce
Soy sauce
Teriyaki sauce
Dry vermouth

Refrigerator Essentials

Mayonnaise
Dijon mustard
Ketchup
Barbecue sauce
Maple syrup
Salsa
Hoisin sauce
Asian chili sauce
Indian curry paste (Madras is our favourite)
Anchovies (look for the ones packed in oil in little jars)
Black olives
Parmesan cheese (buy a block, not grated)
Tomato paste (look for Italian paste sold in tubes)
Buttermilk

Baking Needs

All-purpose flour
Whole wheat flour
Baking soda
Baking powder
Oatmeal (ideally large-flake, not instant)
Cornmeal
Cornstarch
Natural bran
Wheat germ
White sugar
Brown sugar (light and dark)
Icing sugar
Honey
Molasses
Dried fruits (apricots, cranberries, raisins,
    dates, etc.)
Crystallized ginger
Desiccated coconut
Nuts and seeds (almonds, pecans, walnuts,
    sunflower, etc.)
Chocolate (high-quality bittersweet,
    and semisweet chips)
Cocoa powder (Dutch-process and regular)
Unflavoured gelatin powder
Vanilla extract (real, not imitation)
Almond extract
Peanut or other nut butters
Applesauce (unsweetened)

Dried Herbs and Spices
(A long list, so we'll stick with the essentials)

Basil
Bay leaves
Black peppercorns
Cayenne pepper
Cinnamon
Ground coriander
Ground cumin
Hot pepper flakes
Nutmeg
Oregano
Paprika (we like the smoked kind)
Salt (kosher or sea)
Thyme

Canned Goods and Dry Goods

Canned solid white tuna packed in water
Canned Italian plum tomatoes
Canned beans (black beans, white beans, kidney
    beans, Mexican red beans, chickpeas etc.)
Canned coconut milk (make sure coconut is
    the first ingredient listed)
Low-sodium, MSG-free chicken or vegetable
    stocks in Tetra Paks, cans or concentrate
Pasta (spaghetti, farfalle, alphabet, macaroni, etc.)
Asian noodles (rice stick, ramen, soba, etc.)
Rice (basmati, brown, arborio, etc.)
Dried lentils (brown, du Puy, red)
Couscous

Resources

Parenting Books

Ellyn Satter, *Child of Mine: Feeding with Love and Good Sense*, Bull Publishing Co., 1991.
We love Ellyn Satter's approach and would recommend any of her books. *Child of Mine* is a must for new parents and an informative read for anyone facing feeding issues of any kind.

Adele Faber and Elaine Mazlish, *How to Talk So Kids will Listen and Listen So Kids Will Talk*, Avon Books, 1999.
A classic in talking to your kids.

Barbara Coloroso, *Kids are Worth It! Giving Your Child the Gift of Inner Discipline*, Penguin Canada, 2001.
Are you a jellyfish, a brick wall or a backbone parent? Find out by reading this book.

Jane Nelson, *Positive Discipline: The Classic Guide to Helping Children Develop Self-discipline, Responsibility, Co-operation and Problem Solving Skills*, Ballantine Books, 2006.
A common sense how-to that will hopefully quell the yelling and make your family work better as a team.

Feeding Baby Books

Brenda Bradshaw and Dr. Lauren Donaldson Bramley, *The Baby's Table: Over 100 Easy, Healthy and Homemade Recipes for the Pickiest, Most Deserving Eaters on the Planet*, Random House Canada, 2004.
Handy charts and recipes make this a good starter book.

Daina Kalnins and Joanne Saab, *Better Baby Food: Your Essential Guide to Nutrition, Feeding and Cooking for All Babies and Toddlers*, Robert Rose, 2001
A pretty dry read but has all the basic baby food recipes and has the weight of Sick Children's Hospital behind it.

Martha and David Kimmel, *Mommy Made and Daddy Too: Home Cooking for a Healthy Baby & Toddler*, Bantam Books, 2000.
This book, which has gone through a few editions, is a good resource on making your own baby food.

Websites

www.aap.org
American Association of Pediatrics. A comprehensive site covering all sorts of emotional and physical health issues.

www.caringforkids.cps.ca
Canadian Paediatric Society. Answers to health questions, position papers for doctors, as well as an up-to-date list of product recalls and warnings affecting kids.

www.cooksthesaurus.com
A great site if you have questions about substitutions, types of cuisine or you just have to know more about an obscure ingredient.

www.epicurious.com
The best, most trustworthy, most extensive recipe collection on the web.

www.hc-sc.gc.ca
Health Canada's site. Check here for Canada's Health guide, as well as government recommendations for nutritional standards, safety and advice.

www.literarymama.com
Literary Mama. Because we like to read as well as eat.

www.parentcentre.com
One of the first and still incredibly comprehensive sites for any parent's questions.

www.safe4kids.ca
For parents of kids with anaphylactic allergies.

www.todaysparent.com
The site for the excellent Canadian magazine is a good resource for recipes, feeding babies and all things parent.

Acknowledgements

Much thanks to our mothers' groups, book clubs, supper clubs and all the moms and dads at the playgrounds, school functions and everywhere else who answered our questions, told us their frustrations and let us in on their lives. And an especially big thanks to those who tested recipes and gave us great feedback.

To Alison Fryer and Jennifer Grange at the Cookbook Store in Toronto for their knowledgeable input and encouragement.

To parenting guru Beverley Cathcart-Ross, pediatrician Dr. Patricia Neelands and nutritionist Rosie Schwartz, whose common sense and wise words calm our neuroses and inspire us to do better, tomorrow.

We are especially indebted to Hilary McMahon, our agent, who immediately understood the concept of this book. To Tanya Trafford, our acquiring editor at Random House, who knows all about picky eaters and went above and beyond to get this book together. And Kendall Anderson, our project editor, who took on the tough job of stewarding us through the process with skill and diplomacy.

Jenna Muirhead-Warren, our talented photographer whose photos brilliantly illustrate the joy and pain of feeding kids.

To Lucy Waverman, whose advice and knowledge run as an undercurrent through the book. We love and thank her for all her time and insight.

Emma would like to thank her friends, first readers and good listeners: Elizabeth, Catherine, Ijeoma, Charlie, and her sister, Katie. Her parents and in-laws always gave a hand or an hour, when needed. But none of it would be possible without her in-home tech support person, cake decorator, most diplomatic editor, biggest advocate and partner at the table: Micah. And to Zachary, Noah and Talia, who show her every day how to love, play and sometimes even eat with joyous abandon.

Eshun would like to thank Amy and Lindsay for publishing first and showing her it could be done, and all the friends and family who believed in the project from the start. And she'd like to thank James, who willingly ate a year's worth of trial recipes, kept the kids out of the kitchen while the work was being done, and knew when a night of takeout was in order. To Moira, who she hopes will benefit from all she has learned about feeding children. And to Max and Rory, her inspiration and true test subjects, who learned to sit at the table without tears when faced with unfamiliar foods.

Index